What People Are Saying About *Baby Sing & Sign*

Baby Sing & Sign™ is such a natural way for parents to encourage physical contact, interaction and language development with their children. I hope all parents take the opportunity to use this joyful and interactive tool that Anne Meeker Miller has lovingly developed!

> – Terry Busch, R.N.C., M.S.
> Coordinator, Parent and Family Education
> Shawnee Mission Medical Center
> Overland Park, Kansas

I am a firm believer in signing and singing with babies and did so with my daughter from the very beginning. I only wish I would have had your book instead of the one I used. *Baby Sing & Sign*™ is easy to read and enjoyable. I also loved your connection of literature to the signs – the teacher in me says: "Way to go!"

> – Amy Scavuzzo
> Kindergarten Teacher
> Overland Park, Kansas

We often include the *Clap Your Hands* CD as part of our morning routine and can count on the songs to engage us each time we listen, sing and play along. The music provides a fun framework and inspiration for constructive play with our thirteen-month-old daughter, Ava. And, to quote my husband as he "hops along like a bunny" with Ava, "It's a hoot!"

> – Kate

Love this child-centered approach to learning. Thanks for the homemade toy ideas. The music is absolutely delightful as well!

> – Craig

Seeing your child sign for the first time is such an exciting experience. My little boy loved the interactive music and play activities so much! I also appreciated the inexpensive toy ideas. Our family loves *Baby Sing & Sign*™!

> – Susan

Baby Sing & Sign™ is one fun baby party! The music has encouraged my daughter's language development greatly.

> – Lindsay

This multisensory approach to music and sign language encourages parents to give their children choices and allows them to explore their world. As an occupational therapist and a mother, I love the built-in repetition. I also love all of the practical ideas for making inexpensive instruments and toys!

> – Nicole

Learning the signs and songs together with my grandson makes everything so much easier to remember and use with baby daily. We play the CD every day, and Quinten's face lights up each time. He starts clapping as soon as he hears the music.

> – Susan

The *Baby Sing & Sign™* program has provided a strong foundation for my daughter and me to communicate. I love all your great ideas for homemade toys!

– Cathy

Great integration of signs and songs! Jake started clapping his hands to the music right away. He absolutely loves the songs on the music CD. He sits and stares at the stereo in anticipation when we put the music on!

– Jennifer

I love the book lists included with each chapter. I also appreciate the emphasis on fun and creativity. This program has been highly beneficial for my child. "Way to go," *Baby Sing & Sign™*!

– Megan

I love the book and CD! We play the CD almost every day, sometimes a couple of times a day, and my twins, Mason & McKenna, love it! They are starting to use their hands more and are getting close to signing some words like "more" and "ball." Even if I don't have the CD or book near me, I sing the songs and use props to sing. They always start smiling and looking at me like they know the music and start moving, clapping, etc. Thank you so much for this wonderful tool to introduce language and interaction for my ten-month-old twins.

– Kim

Taylor now signs during her tantrums to let us know what she wants. She also loves the CD when we're in the car. Her favorite signs are "more" and "eat." It has really helped me feel comfortable when she is going to be away from me, I just tell our caretakers what sign means what and they're good to go. *Baby Sing & Sign™* is a wonderful program!

– Heather

My son loves the songs and CD. When we were driving back from the grandparents and he started to get a little fussy, I started singing the songs with him and he started smiling and just listened to me. Thanks for a great program!

– Crystal

What an amazing program! Our whole family has jumped on the *Baby Sing & Sign™* bandwagon. Our six-year-old daughter is teaching grandma to sign. We love this program.

– Katherine

I love the book. It's awesome! How could there be a better baby gift?!

– Stephanie

BABY SING & SIGN™

A Play-Filled
Language Development Program
for Hearing Infants and Toddlers

Anne Meeker Miller, Ph.D.

SECOND EDITION

Love Language Publications
Olathe, Kansas

Publisher's Cataloging-in-Publication

Miller, Anne Meeker.
    Baby sing & sign : a play-filled language development program for hearing infants and toddlers / Anne Meeker Miller ; "A sign of success" stories by Anne Meeker Miller & Carrie Kent ; illustrations by Jeff Petrie ; photography by Amy Martin. – 2nd ed.
      p. cm.
      ISBN 0-9749924-1-0
      LCCN 2004098386

    1. American Sign Language–Study and teaching (Early childhood) I. Kent, Carrie. II. Title. III. Title: Baby sing and sign

    HV2474.M537 2005   419'.7083
                       QBI04-200497

Written by Anne Meeker Miller, Ph.D.
"A Sign of Success" Stories written by Anne Meeker Miller & Carrie Kent
Photography by Amy Martin
Illustrated by Jeff Petrie
Music transcribed by Jan Holthus
Design by Kim Tappan/Tappan Design
Printed in the United States of America
Second edition: March 2005

www.babysingandsign.com

Baby Sing & Sign™ is a registered trademark of Love Language™ Publications

Disclaimer of Liability

The author wishes to thank the following for permission to include copyrighted material:

Hyperion for the excerpt from *The World According to Mister Rogers* by Fred Rogers. Copyright ©2003 Family Communications, Inc. Reprinted by permission of Hyperion. All Rights Reserved.

GIA Publications, Inc. for "Lady, Lady" in *Lullabies* (2000), "The Little Mouse Goes Creeping" in *Wiggles & Tickles* (2000), and "Roll the Ball" in *The Book of Simple Songs and Circles* (1996). John M. Feierabend compiled all three collections.

Harvard University Press for "Miss Mary Jane" in *On the Trail of Negro Folk Songs* by Dorothy Scarborough (1925).

The Seeger family for "Clap Your Hands" in *American Folksongs for Children* by Ruth Crawford Seeger (1948).

The Writers' Union of Canada for "Sally Go 'Round the Sun" in Edith Fowke's folksong collection, *Sally Go 'Round the Sun* (Doubleday & Company, 1969).

A Tribute to
Ruth Crawford Seeger

Ruth Crawford Seeger (1901-1953), mother of Pete, Peggy and Mike Seeger, was a premier pianist and music scholar and one of the first women composers of her day to be taken seriously. She collected and transcribed many of the familiar folksongs of our country and contributed to the folk music anthologies of Carl Sandburg and John and Alan Lomax. Her own *American Folk Songs for Children* remains a valuable resource for music teachers of young children.

Mrs. Seeger – or "Dio," as she was affectionately called by her family – is a model for women today who try to combine their life's work with motherhood. Said daughter, Peggy: "Our house echoed with love, clean clothes, good food, freedom, and evenings of singing." Ruth Seeger's legacy endures through her musical contributions and the treasured memories of her children and grandchildren.

To learn more about the life and music of this extraordinary woman, read *Ruth Crawford Seeger: A Composer's Search for American Music* (Oxford University Press, 2000) by Judith Tick.

Mrs. Seeger sings and plays with her young students.

(Photo reprinted with permission of the Seeger family.)

DEDICATION

I dedicate this book to my mother,
Mary Anne (1935-2000), and my father, Don.
They made me the "folk-singin' mama" that I am today.

– Anne

A portion of the proceeds from the sale of this book
goes to support children's causes.

CONTENTS

Resources

About the Author

Contributors

Acknowledgments

Product Information

Order Form

Music CD Information

It's the things we play with
and the people who help us play
that make a great difference in our lives.

– Mr. Fred Rogers

INTRODUCTION

Kevin and his mother are playing a guessing game. Various versions of this game are repeated dozens of times throughout the day. Kevin is a determined young man of thirteen months who wants something in the kitchen cabinet, and Mom is trying her best to figure out what that might be. She begins to list from memory all of the items in the cabinet that might be desirable to him: cookie, apple, milk, cracker. With each incorrect guess, Kevin's frustration level elevates. Pretty soon he adds foot stomping and loud squealing to his pointing game. His discontent is obvious, and his mother's frustration is growing.

Babies and toddlers are invested in their independence from the start. They are pleased that their known universe appears to be revolving around them, and they enjoy the numerous sources of entertainment and enlightenment the adults in their lives provide. They truly believe their babble is intelligible to your adult ear, and try with all their baby might to communicate using their repertoire of facial expressions, body language and vocalizations. Unfortunately, as illustrated in the example of Kevin and his mother, this process can fall short of the communication needs for both parent and child.

Fortunately, there are ways to bridge this early communication gap. Long before their vocal mechanisms are mature enough to verbalize, babies can learn to communicate their wants and needs using gestures or signs. Sign language supports the natural development of the ability to speak. Babies who learn to sign experience less frustration and often verbalize sooner than their peers and, most important, sign language strengthens the bond between caregiver and child.

The program described in this book is a unique version of other instructional approaches to baby sign language by using music and picture books to structure the teaching and practice of the signs. The method is an outgrowth of my work as a music therapist for a public school system in the Kansas City area. Asked by a colleague to explore the use of music as a way to help infants and toddlers learn to sign, I found that music proved to be an engaging and motivating tool. Babies as well as parents were responsive, and we observed wonderful attention during our music activities.

The *Baby Sing & Sign*™ program is the result of my teaching experiences with infants and toddlers. Young children and their caregivers – parents, grandparents, nannies and others – have enjoyed the songs, signs and play in a group setting by participating in *Baby Sing & Sign*™ classes. The purpose of writing this book was to share this playful musical approach to sign language instruction with babies and toddlers who spend time at home or in childcare.

The music written or adapted for this book has a distinctively folksy feel. The melodies are simple but musically interesting. Used as a language development program for infants, the recommended age range is from birth to two years. However, the tunes comprise a repertoire that can become a part of the entire family's tradition. The songs are inviting to children of all ages.

With each song presented in the book, you and your child will learn new signs and practice musical as well as communication skills that are playful and developmentally appropriate. *Baby Sing & Sign*™ utilizes materials readily at hand that are easily assimilated into your daily routine. No special equipment or training is needed. All that is necessary is a willingness to play and an interest in allowing baby to direct his or her learning adventure!

About This Book

This Introduction gives a brief overview of the *Baby Sing & Sign*™ program, followed by answers to frequently asked questions about sign language, music and young children. "Getting Started" gives you the basics for teaching children how to sing and sign and illustrates the hand formations that will be used throughout the book.

Chapters 1 through 14 – the centerpiece of the book – appear in the order of the playlist on the *Baby Sing & Sign*™ music CD (found inside the back cover). Each song chapter consists of the following elements.

The section "Tips for Introducing the Song" gives ideas for how to teach the song as well as the signs listed as "Words to Learn." "More Musical Fun" describes additional activities designed to extend music and sign language learning while helping to maintain the child's interest.

"Games to Play" shows you how to make toys and play games with materials readily at hand in order to practice the sign language vocabulary. The activities can be customized to suit the developmental stage of your child, and help children grow in other areas, such as fine-motor and problem-solving skills. As a supplement to the infinite number and types of commercial toys available, homemade toys are creative and inexpensive. Utilizing homemade toys for play also teaches your child that toys do not have to come from a store.

"Books to Read" lists a series of books recommended for infants and toddlers that fit the musical theme and vocabulary of a given chapter. Let this list be a starting point as you explore other titles at your local library or bookstore. Early reading experiences are wonderful for babies and toddlers and set the stage for their future literacy. Book engagement is an important predictor of reading success, and another effective way to practice sign language vocabulary. Take care not to overwhelm your child with sign language to avoid spoiling the closeness and security the child feels with you as you snuggle and read. Add signs gradually to the reading of books as you introduce them to your child. Repetition is necessary for learning the books as well as understanding and using sign language.

"A Sign of Success" stories share thoughts about child development and parenting, and relate the experiences of parents and other caregivers who have participated in *Baby Sing & Sign*™ on their own or in classes. These vignettes are arranged in order of complexity – from the importance of being a patient teacher to the wonders of children expressing themselves through music and sign language. In several of the chapters, the Sign of Success stories are accompanied by a list of resources for those who would like to read more on a given topic.

Finally, in the back of the book you will find lists of books and websites about language development and music for young children. There are also brief summaries of articles about the benefits of sign language and music with babies and toddlers, as well as a glossary of terms. Whenever possible, everyday language has been used throughout the book. However, some terms commonly used in the discussion of language and child development are included where necessary to ensure clarity and precision. These more "technical" terms are defined in the glossary.

Note Regarding Homemade Toys and Other Items

When making and using homemade toys, the safety and well-being of your child is the first concern. Please read the following points carefully before proceeding with any of the homemade toys described.

- Homemade toys have not been subject to mandatory toy safety regulations. Please use your best judgment when preparing and playing with these items.

- Infants and toddlers must be supervised at all times when using toys.

- Babies put things in their mouths. Be sure toys are too large for them to choke on, are non-toxic and have smooth surfaces.

- As with all toys, check homemade toys often to be certain they are safe for play.

How to Use This Book

This book is much like Thanksgiving dinner: it is not intended to be consumed in one sitting. The best plan for using, enjoying and benefiting from *Baby Sing & Sign*™ with your child is to take the songs and signs one at a time. Sing a tune with and without the CD until you know the lyrics well. Once both you and your child are familiar with the song, find the signs in the corresponding chapter and introduce them to your child. The suggested games and books can be added to enhance the fun – in moderation and with good humor – as you proceed.

Baby Sing & Sign™ is a process that allows parents and caregivers to capture the child's attention with music and teach sign language in such a playful way that children never realize they are learning a new skill. The program is designed to fit into your daily life with children and is meant to enhance – rather than complicate – your daily routine.

Conventions Used in This Book

Here are some organizational features that have been used throughout the book:

- The pronouns "he" and "she" are used alternately to refer to babies and toddlers who will use the program.

- Italics are used for safety reminders.

- The book refers to parents and caregivers when describing caring adults who will use the program with children. Given the growing diversity of families, modify the song texts and other activities as needed to fit your family structure.

Frequently Asked Questions

To help you get a better feel for the nature and benefits of *Baby Sing & Sign*™, I have solicited the opinions of some wise and experienced caregivers who have used the program, in addition to my own comments and observations.

Q: What is *Baby Sing & Sign*™?

Baby Sing & Sign™ is an enrichment program for infants and toddlers that is equal parts music, baby sign language and play-based activities. The *Baby Sing & Sign*™ program supports the natural development of a child's language skills as she begins to make meaning of information, ideas and social interactions she experiences in her world. The music activities promote the child's emerging abilities to respond to the melodic, rhythmic and expressive elements of music. Music is also used to facilitate the practice of sign language vocabulary and playful exchanges between caregiver and child. The ultimate benefit is an enhanced bond between parent or caregiver and the child.

Q: Will my child still learn to speak if I teach him to sign?

Yes! Sign language provides an alternative to speech for children at a point in their physical development when their vocal mechanism is not mature enough to speak intelligibly. The ability to communicate through gesture gives the child experience in mastering the reciprocity or "taking turns" of language, as well as the gratification of expressing needs that are then met by caregivers. In my experience, children whom I have taught to sign stop signing words once they can say them clearly enough to be understood.

Kreg signs THANK YOU.

"We signed with Josie and Max. My biggest concern was that our kids wouldn't talk because they relied so heavily on signs. But that was not the case. Our parent educator was amazed at Josie's vocabulary, and people still are. Max was even more advanced than Josie. At eighteen months, Max could say anything."

– Stephanie

Q: I thought sign language was only used to communicate with people who are deaf. Why should I use sign language with my hearing child?

Babies have the ability to understand and communicate long before they are physically able to speak. Using signed gestures enables babies to "tell" caregivers what they want and need, and therefore, eliminates a lot of guess work and frustration. Using the *Baby Sing & Sign*™ program creates a language- and music-rich learning environment.

"I look at my friends who have toddlers, and I believe they are doing their child a disservice by NOT teaching them to sign. As a parent, my job is to help my child adapt and succeed in this world. By providing him with the means to communicate, I am validating my son's needs and desires. At eighteen months, Matthew is confident and patient and knows how to use the communication tools he has been given to his benefit."

– Casey

Q: Who can use the *Baby Sing & Sign*™ program?

Parents, grandparents, teachers, babysitters and daycare providers can all use the program. The song material is appropriate for children from birth through the primary-grade levels. The program is ideal for any child or parent with an interest in learning to sign.

Experience in sign and song is an added benefit for children in home daycare or childcare facilities. Parents can be encouraged to play with the child at home to help the child thoroughly master the skills.

"I run a home daycare business. I use Baby Sing & Sign™ with my children each day. It is part of our routine. I care for children of all ages, and they all enjoy the songs, signs and activities. I see offering the program to my families as another attractive feature for parents to consider when they are choosing childcare."

– Robin

Q: Why do you use music to teach babies sign language?

Music is a great tool for teaching sign vocabulary because it is inherently interesting and engaging to children. Active participation in music from an early age helps realize children's musical potential. In addition, both music and language give babies experience in detecting and organizing the patterns of sound, helping them to be focused and attentive listeners from an early age.

Q: How does it feel to sign with babies and toddlers?

Enabling children to express their desires to the people who create the happiness and contentment in their world is a profoundly moving experience. It is amazing to see such little people direct the outcome of their daily activities by shaping their small hands. For both child and caregiver, their special "love language" is a powerful means of strengthening their bond. Sign language gives the caregiver a greater appreciation of the child's naturally developing ability to master communication.

"I wasn't convinced that my son would catch on to signed communication. I started using signs in my conversation with him when he was six months old. He didn't actually start signing until after his first birthday. I asked him if he wanted more water, and he signed ALL-DONE. It was such a small gesture – just a flick of his wrists – but I was blown away by the power of it! It made him feel so grown up to be able to communicate with his siblings. It was truly a satisfying experience for all of us. I wish I had signed with my other children."

– Bob

Q: What is the best age for my child to start the *Baby Sing & Sign*™ program?

I recommend that you sing and play music to children from the first weeks of their lives. Babies can actually hear a muted version of the world from inside the womb by the third trimester. My newborn son became noticeably calmer when I played recordings of my school choir at his bedtime. I believe he remembered the songs from listening to the choir rehearse during my pregnancy.

The beauty of the *Baby Sing & Sign*™ program is that it grows with the child. Make music a natural part of your lives together. Take your time just singing and enjoying the songs during the first months of the child's life. When baby is old enough to sit up, or around six months, you can begin introducing signs gradually as a part of your music making.

The child will begin to make sense of your gestures and start accumulating this knowledge in his or her baby brain until typically age ten to twelve months. You should then look for the child to begin using the gestures in conversation with you. However, please remember that each child is unique and may not conform to a predictable pattern for development in this or any other area. The *Baby Sing & Sign*™ program can also be beneficial to young children who are verbalizing. Gesture is a natural extension of musical expression for children.

"Breast-feeding and sign teaching were similar parenting experiences for me. Some children take to breast-feeding and never want to be weaned, while others prefer the bottle from the start and want little to do with the breast. I taught both of my children to sign using the Baby Sing & Sign™ program. They both enjoyed the music and language play. However, one of my children ended up signing a lot while the other seemed to under-stand my gestures but didn't actually sign to me very often. Both started talking at about the same age, and we still enjoy singing the songs and playing the games. The music was as beneficial as the baby sign for our family."

— Karen

Hannah signs BOOK.

Q: How do I hold my child to teach her to sign?

I suggest that you sing the songs to children first. Where does baby respond best to your music play: sitting in your lap and bouncing, watching you at bath or mealtime, in the rocking chair at night or while being held and dancing to one of your favorite tunes? Experiment with the best ways to maintain the child's eye contact and interest. This will set the stage and guide you as you begin to introduce signs.

"My child is walking now and I can never seem to keep up with her! I find the best times for us to do our sign and music play are when she is in the high chair and at bedtime when we are snuggling in to read a book. I make our music and sign play sessions short and let her direct what song we sing and how we sing it – slow and smooth, or fast and bouncy!"

— Roberta

Q: I have twin infants and can hardly manage the parenting demands of their daily care. Can *Baby Sing & Sign*™ benefit parents like us who are overworked and overwhelmed?

Parenting is not for wimps. The demands and responsibilities that go with the job, compounded by frequent sleep deprivation, tax even the hardiest of us. But we do have one thing going for us: babies are fairly predictable in their needs and desires. They crave structure and predictability. They strive for independence, while simultaneously refusing to let go of your pant leg … and they like the fruity baby food better than any of the pureed green vegetables.

Rather than adding new responsibilities, the *Baby Sing & Sign*™ program can help make parenting and caregiving easier. Singing and playing is embedded in the rituals of your daily life: mealtime, car rides, bath and bedtime. And since the music and sign language activities engage and interest children, they come to associate listening to your singing voice or the music CD with all things good and playful. *Baby Sing & Sign*™ is just the "spoonful of sugar" Mary Poppins was singing about when it was time for her charges to clean the playroom. Music becomes instrumental (no music pun intended) in getting children willingly involved in the tasks of your life together.

Jaclynn signs BUNNY.

The program can also help children transition from one activity to another. For example, you can sing and sign your way from playing with toys in the warmth and security of the family room to riding in the car to the grocery store. By redirecting baby from the reality of the dreaded shopping trip to the enjoyment of playing and singing with you in the car, you are able to minimize tantrums and discontent.

Singing and signing does not require any special effort. Playing the music CD while attending to children is a simple multi-tasking activity that enables you and baby to enjoy the songs. Once you have become familiar with your new musical repertoire, it is easy to sing the songs as you show the signs and you can change the lyrics to suit your fancy, making them all your own if you choose.

Babies who are able to communicate their desire for a drink, a snack or a hug are less frustrated. Caregivers who are able to understand their child's needs and desires are also less frustrated. Ninety percent of parents surveyed named frustration at not knowing what their child wanted as a primary source of stress in their lives. The other ten percent were too sleep-deprived to be able to hold a pencil and write legibly on the survey form!

"I understand being overworked and overstressed, as I am the mother of thirteen-month-old twins. This can be very challenging! I try to use the signs as much as possible. It does not take any added effort. The twins are trying to verbalize what they want, and I help them by giving them the sign. Both of them have used signs for MORE and WANT. They have the biggest smiles when I repeat back to them what they signed. The rewards are amazing."

– Melissa

"I have an active toddler and am in the final trimester of my pregnancy. Eric wears me out! I was dreading our drive to see my family for Thanksgiving, as my son doesn't tolerate his car seat very well. I anticipated five hours of screaming! We brought along our Baby Sing & Sign™ music CD and our son was happy for the entire car trip. The familiar tunes and the memory of the music games he and I play seemed to provide the comfort and interest he needed. He is an attentive listener when we sing or play the music, and we just saw him sign STOP and ALL-DONE for the first time when were singing 'The Walking Song' last week."

– Susan

Q: Did you make up the signs you teach?

The *Baby Sing & Sign*™ program uses American Sign Language (ASL) signs, but some of the gestures have been modified so that they are better suited to the fine-motor abilities of babies. I purposefully use this widely accepted system of signed communication as it will enable many children to use their signing skills when they are older with peers who are hearing impaired or deaf in school, church or other social activities.

Babies will not produce all the signs exactly as suggested in the book. Always accept their best "approximation" or attempt to sign, and treat it as the intended word. There are pictures of a young child signing modified versions of the ASL signs throughout the book. These are just examples of ways your child may perform the signs you teach.

Q: I also have older children. How can I involve them in *Baby Sing & Sign*™?

Involving the entire family in *Baby Sing & Sign*™ is recommended. Babies need to see what the signs look like on all of the hands in the household. They also benefit from observing signed conversation between family members. Older siblings are important role models, and the youngest children will work hard to imitate the behaviors of "big" sisters or brothers.

The musical material for the program is fun and interesting for children of all ages. Traditionally, folk music has been passed down from one generation to the next through "oral transmission." That is, grandparents and parents sang to their children, and those children sang the same songs to their children and grandchildren when they grew up. Each family made the folk tunes their own by adding words or altering the melody. This active participation in music stands in stark contrast to the typical music participation today. We have become a nation of musical consumers, passively experiencing music by limiting ourselves to just listening.

Giving children songs they can sing to their own babies when they become parents some day is a wonderful gift. Activities that you share are memories in the making. Try to make singing and signing a family affair.

"I taught my daughter to sign, and she really took off with it. My second child, Sam, was slower to catch on. My daughter appointed herself the 'sign tutor' for her little brother. It was neat to watch her patiently instructing her brother in the hand shapes and their meanings. Sam responded thanks to my daughter and now has a sign vocabulary of twenty words. I love watching my children communicate with one another in their special language. My wife and I have benefited from my daughter's efforts, as Sam signs with us all now."

— Dennis

Q: I love rock-and-roll music, but when I look at the assortment of music CDs at the store produced specifically for children, I am overwhelmed and confused. What type of music should I play for my child?

It is important to involve babies in music making that is suited to their developmental needs. The growth and development of the brain depends on the quality and quantity of interactions children have with their environment, and for newborns much of this input comes through their ears. Listening to the sounds of the world and learning to turn toward a sound source comes as children are able to integrate what they see, hear and feel.

Quiet listening to a variety of music styles can be a positive experience for infants. Take care to control the loudness of the music, and try to find music that is soothing and contains predictable patterns that the baby can begin to organize and analyze in inquisitive baby fashion. Baby music should ideally contain a mixture of simple, yet interesting material so that, with repetition, the baby will recognize and remember the tune. This book suggests ways to modify tunes that become familiar to baby in order to keep her musical mind engaged and growing.

The *Baby Sing & Sign*™ program provides active experiences in music and language play. When choosing music for listening to or singing with children, consider the following:

- Do the songs engage the child's mind, motor skills and imagination?

- Are the elements (rhythm, melody, lyrics) and instruments the child hears simple, yet interesting?

- Can my child and I sing the songs and enjoy ourselves without having to play the recording?

- Are the tunes open-ended enough to allow our family or daycare to experiment with the rhythm, tempo and words to make them our own?

Songs written for young children with adult listening preferences in mind have little to do with the musical needs of their intended audience. There are also songs that profess to meet the musical needs of babies and toddlers, but would bore any self-respecting youngster to tears.

Dr. John Feierabend has written several wonderful music books for young children (see the resources in the back of the book). He believes a song should be "delicious after many repetitions." If music is the food of love, play on!

"I am a musician by profession, and am embarrassed to say that I didn't sing very much with my baby. The baby songs I knew bored me. I couldn't get excited about singing 'Twinkle, Twinkle Little Star' with my daughter. I needed songs that were interesting to me in order to get excited about singing with my baby. The songs in this book were playful and fun for us both."

– Bruce

Anthony signs CHEESE.

"My daughter especially loved 'Mommy Go 'Round the Sun' from the Baby Sing & Sign™ *music CD. I sang her a special version with verses for every one of her friends and family members. She loved that we had our own special song. Of course, once you create a new song, you will need to include everyone each time you sing it. This can be both good and bad – good when I am trying to get all of her parts washed thoroughly in the bathtub, but bad when I am in a public place and don't feel like serenading everyone in the room!"*

– Kirsten

"I began singing to Lana before she was born. My father was always singing and playing music as I grew up, so it just seemed natural. She seemed to respond to any music. I was a dance teacher at the time I was pregnant. Whenever music would play, I would feel my daughter move. After she was born, music was a daily and nightly ritual. She still falls asleep to music at night and her brother does the same thing. We sing in the car, on walks – any time! Singing and signing is an easy and natural way to teach your children language skills. It is also fun!"

– Norma

Q: Are there other children who might benefit from the *Baby Sing & Sign*™ program?

Children with special needs often lack the oral-motor or language-processing ability to speak. The program would be an engaging and simple way to introduce sign language to them.

"Anna suffered a massive brain hemorrhage in utero (cause unknown) and as a result has hydrocephalus, cerebral palsy, cortical visual impairment, as well as feeding and speech problems. Although her ability to understand language has developed typically, her ability to speak has progressed very little over the last two years. I know

your program probably focuses on typically developing kids. However, I think sign and music are even more important to kids with developmental delays, as they have both been so instrumental in Anna's development. Anna absolutely loves music and has since the day she was born. It is often the only thing that will calm her during stressful times. We often use music as a reward when trying to teach Anna new skills. It is a positive motivator for her because she loves it so much. Although Anna has limited use of her hands and is almost blind, she has learned about seven signs thus far, which have been invaluable. If a child with multiple disabilities like Anna can learn signs, any typically developing child can learn signs!"

– Diane

Children who are adopted internationally can experience delays in speech due to language differences and the lack of a nurturing and stimulating environment during their infancy. Children often respond quickly to sign and song. Musical experiences are a wonderful way to introduce our culture and customs. Sign language bridges the language gap between parent and child, and jump-starts their bonding process.

"Our daughter was thirteen months when we adopted her, so she already had a good start on learning Mandarin. When she came to live with us, she didn't talk at all for quite some time. She definitely understood the gestures we used with her and responded incredibly to music. I don't consider myself to be a very good singer, but she was always in better spirits when I would sing to her. We believe she now talks better than most three-year-olds."

– Sharon and Ken

Hannah signs APPLE.

"We adopted Faith when she was ten months old. She understands what we say to her, but it has taken a year for her speech to develop. We have tried different things to help her language develop, but believe sign language has been the most effective. Our daycare taught her to use MORE and that has given her a way to let us know her desires besides just grunting! She loves music and begins to move and smile immediately when we sing with her. Sign language and music have been invaluable to us for helping Faith with language learning and making the transition to our family."

– Pam

Getting Started

- Teach one sign at a time. Progress slowly so that your child can learn "deeply" the sign you are presenting, and move from simply recognizing the sign to comprehending its meaning.

- Always speak as well as sign. You are teaching your child to respond to both your verbal and signed communication.

- You may use either hand to form the signs.

- Use facial expressions that reinforce what you are trying to communicate.

- Give your baby adequate time to respond before repeating signs.

- Continue to sign to your child even if he does not sign to you. Although you may not see your child forming signs and using them to communicate with you, he most likely understands the words and signs you use to communicate with him.

- Look for an approximation or "best try" as your child attempts to imitate the signs you teach.

- Be positive and encouraging. Don't forget to have fun!

 **WAVING**

Megan will demonstrate signs based on American Sign Language (ASL).

Lana will show some of the possible modifications a child might make to the ASL signs.

Hand Formations

The adult model throughout the book demonstrates the vocabulary using American Sign Language (ASL). For the purpose of teaching you basic baby sign vocabulary, here are some hand formations that will be used. When referred to in the book, hand formations appear in italics.

Flat hand or closed fingers

Gathered fingertips

Closed two fingers

Open two fingers

Closed fist

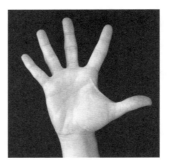
Open fingers

Note: Teaching finger spelling and extensive ASL vocabulary is beyond the scope of this book. Refer to other sources for more information.

The Secrets of Success with Singing and Signing

- Remember: Repetition is good. Repetition is good. Repetition is good. You will undoubtedly tire of the songs and activities long before your child. The goal is to support your child's typical language development process by teaching signed communication skills. That requires practice.

- Make your sign teaching a natural part of your day. Language learning requires a meaningful context.

- Let your child direct you in selecting signs that have importance for her. Your child may have an affinity for playing BALL or adore your family's DOG. Start with what she cares about most.

- Take "baby steps" in incorporating the ideas from this book into your child's life. Play with a sign and a song for as long as it takes for both of you to feel confident you have mastered the material.

- Remind yourself often that the real reason for doing baby sign language and music with your child is to have fun!

The goal behind this book is to create activities that you can enjoy with your child while connecting with him in a more meaningful way. While research does suggest that the use of sign can enhance the overall communication skills for children, this may not be the case for every child.

The activities and information in this book are in no way intended to substitute for the expertise and assistance of a speech-language pathologist, and are not intended to replace speech or language therapy. If you have any concerns about the development of your child, particularly in the area of communication, please talk to your pediatrician and/or contact your local school district for screening information.

Isaac and mom are "having a ball"
learning to sign BALL!

1
Clap Your Hands

Words To Learn:
MORE, MUSIC

Tips for introducing *Clap Your Hands*

- This joyful, upbeat folk tune requires little explanation. Allow the lyrics to lead you as you move to the music. You can pantomime playing the different instruments you hear during the interlude.

- Babies will need some gentle assistance to perform the claps. You can make the song into a bounce on your lap for babies, jostling them as you stamp your feet and "run with me." See if the child will imitate your head movements on "move your head."

- Sign MUSIC as each instrument plays a solo on the "la" passages of the song.

- Ask your child if she would like MORE "Clap Your Hands." Help her form the sign for MORE with her hands. Thank your child for signing MORE. Then sing the song again from the top!

MORE

Tap *gathered fingertips* of both hands together several times.

Naomi's version of MORE includes one *open hand*. Look for your baby's approximation of the sign you demonstrate.

16

Clap, clap, clap your hands,
Clap your hands together,
Clap, clap, clap your hands,
Clap your hands together.
La la la

2. Stomp, stomp, stomp your feet
3. Move, move, move your head
4. Dance, dance, dance with me
5. Run, run, run with me

American Folk Songs for Children by Ruth Crawford Seeger.
Copyright © 2002 by Mike Seeger
All rights reserved. Adapted by Anne Meeker Miller

More musical fun with *Clap Your Hands*

- The "la" passages in between verses present a good chance for your child to improvise some moves of his own. Observe him to see if he is beginning to anticipate this repeating section of the song. For example, babies may begin to kick their legs or move their arms. Toddlers may alter their movements in expectation of the returning "la's."

- You can pantomime playing the different instruments you hear during the interlude.

- "Clap Your Hands" is a wonderful song to incorporate into the activities of your daily life. There are countless verses you and your child can create: roll the ball, take a bath, or brush your teeth (tooth if it is a small baby). Be sure to sing the "la" passage with enthusiasm!

MUSIC

Wave the palm of one *flat hand* over the other extended arm held with palm up. Sweep hand back and forth from wrist to shoulder.

To simplify the gesture, child may wave arm in the air without crossing her body to her extended arm.

GAMES TO PLAY

Bells on Her Fingers and Bells on His Toes

Materials: elastic, needle and thread, jingle bells, stuffed toy animal

Vocabulary Practice: MUSIC, MORE

Other Benefits: motor skills, awareness of sound

Directions: Sew the ends of the elastic together to form ankle and wrist bracelets. Make sure the elastic is not too tight. Sew jingle bells securely onto the elastic bands. Place the bracelets around the child's ankles and wrists. Play the recording of "Clap Your Hands" and help your baby shake the bells. Provide lots of happy facial expression and giggles. Stop the music and ask your child if she would like MORE?

Hold your child tight and take her for a spin on your dance floor cleared of furniture and other potential obstacles. Tell your child how much you like MUSIC and dancing with her. Be sure to do some gentle dips and spins to maximize the jingles and jangles of the bells. Perhaps a stuffed animal might like to wear the jingle bells and do a fancy dance, too. Let your child "dance" the toy around! NOTE: *As with all the activities described in this book, it is important that adults supervise children carefully to keep them safe as they learn and explore.*

Clapping is a natural way for babies to express pleasure, and one of the first "signs" your child will perform.

Musical Pictures

Materials: trading card plastic protector sheet, index cards, glue, instrument pictures

Vocabulary Practice: MUSIC

Other Benefits: use of pictures to create meaning, focused listening and looking

Directions: Many toddlers enjoy an instrument picture game. Find pictures of the instruments on the Internet or in magazines and paste them onto paper or index cards. Slip the cards into the pockets of a trading card plastic protector sheet. These are inexpensive and can be purchased from an office supply store or your local Wal-Mart. (Buy several, because there are other ways to use them described in this book.)

Some of the instruments you hear on the music CD include guitar, mandolin (small string instrument played like a guitar), flute and violin, in addition to singing. Ask your child to point to MUSIC. Ask him to listen to the MUSIC.

Laundry Basket Swing

Materials: laundry basket, blanket

Vocabulary Practice: MORE, MUSIC

Other Benefits: awareness of cause and effect, social interaction, musical play

Directions: Use blankets to pad a laundry basket to fit the size of your child. Place the child in the basket.

Hold the laundry basket with another adult partner and swing the child gently. Create a melody for a simple lyric such as "swing, swing, swing" to the rhythm of your swinging. Set the child down and ask if she would like MORE swinging? Help your child form the MORE sign. Tell your child "good signing MORE," then continue the swinging game.

Children enjoy practicing their sign language vocabulary with the laundry basket swing game.

BOOKS TO READ

Beaumont, Karen. *Baby Danced the Polka*. New York: Dial Books for Young Readers, 2004.

Cauley, Lorinda. *Clap Your Hands*. New York: Putnam Publications Group, 1992.

Ellwand, David. *Clap Your Hands*. Brooklyn, NY: Handprint Books, 2001.

Gray, Libba Moore. *When Uncle Took the Fiddle*. New York: Orchard Books, 1999.

Guthrie, Woody. *Howdi Do*. Cambridge, MA: Candlewick Press, 2000.

Perkins, Lynne Rae. *Snow Music*. New York: Greenwillow, 2003.

Shields, Carol Diggory. *Saturday Night at the Dinosaur Stomp*. New York: Scholastic, 1997.

Wargin, Kathy-Jo and Katherine Larson. *M Is for Melody*. Farmington Hills, MI: Gale Group, 2004.

Williams, Vera B. *"More, More, More," Said the Baby*. New York: HarperFestival, 1997.

Ziefert, Harriet. *Animal Music*. New York: Houghton Mifflin Company, 1999.

A SIGN OF SUCCESS

The Importance of Early Experience and Receptive Language

Train up a child in the way he should go:
and when he is old, he will not depart from it.

– PROVERBS 22:6

A child's experience in early life is crucial for later cognitive, emotional, physical and psychological development. The same holds true for language. From their earliest days, nothing is more important to babies than the sound of their parent's voice. It is through talking and interacting on a daily basis that their language abilities develop and grow. It's never too early to begin imprinting your baby's brain, so don't feel embarrassed when other shoppers give you odd looks as you push your cart down the grocery store aisle, discussing with your newborn which brand of spaghetti sauce you prefer and why.

That's because receptive language – the ability to understand words – develops before expressive language – the ability to speak and use words. Child development specialists are discovering that even the youngest infants are capable of understanding what is being said to them, even if only through a parent's facial expressions or tone of voice. And by six to eight months of age, most babies understand what certain words mean.

Your child must learn to imitate your actions before she can begin to sign.

Amy began signing to her daughter, Isabella, long before her child had the ability to sign back because she found it was an excellent way to connect symbols to the words she was using with her infant daughter over and over throughout the day. Although Isabella did not sign back for many months, Amy knew her daughter was developing receptive language by the way she would respond to certain signs. For example, when her mother signed MILK or EAT before her morning meal, Isabella would babble with delight and move her hands and feet in a display of happiness. Also, Amy used the sign for HELP whenever she saw Isabella becoming frustrated. The infant would appear to calm down, as if knowing that her mother understood her frustration and would try to help with whatever was distressing her.

Kendall began signing to her son, Isaac, right after he was born. When their son was five months old, she and her husband really focused on sign language, and they believe that Isaac already understands the meaning of the sign ALL-DONE. In addition to her tour of duty as a devoted mom, Kendall has a college degree in early childhood development and works part-time as a consultant helping to support young children with special needs in a local school district.

It is through talking and interacting on a daily basis that children's language abilities develop and grow.

Through her work she was fortunate to meet a student with autism who, at age two, still had no expressive language. Kendall reunited with the student when she was nine and found the child's expressive language had greatly improved. She also discovered that her former student could talk about things she remembered from when she was much younger; another example of how children – any child – can understand language even when they don't participate in it through verbal communication.

So don't feel silly the next time you have a heart-to-heart talk with your infant. She might relate.

2
This Is the Mommy Wiggle

Words To Learn:
MOMMY, DADDY

Words To Review:
MUSIC

Tips for introducing *This Is the Mommy Wiggle*

- You probably remember saying "This Little Piggie" where you touch and wiggle baby's toes. Baby's fingers can wiggle as well. "Wiggles" are popular baby games, and hundreds of them are recorded in American folklore.

- I wrote this updated variation of an old finger play. For example, there is no longer a "short, stout" mother or sister who only plays with dolls. The "baby king" lyric refers to our special name for my third son. Although we tried not to spoil him, he had both of his big brothers doing his bidding from the start.

- You can touch baby's fingers as you share the text, or you can show the baby your fingers. Be sure to sign MOMMY, DADDY and MUSIC as you sing or speak the words.

MOMMY

Place thumb of *open fingers* on chin, then move hand forward.

Child may tap or point to her chin.

This is the **mommy** sweet as can be.
This is the **daddy** who snuggles with me.
This is the sister – she loves to play.
This is the brother who shouts "Hooray!"
This is the baby who thinks she's Queen
[or he's King],
And this is the **song** that they love to sing:
[Sing and sign music] La la la la,
La la la la

Sung to the tune of
"Twinkle, Twinkle Little Star"
Adapted by Anne Meeker Miller

27

More musical fun with *This Is the Mommy Wiggle*

- Babies prefer songs with a quick tempo, so sing lively!

- Try making this wiggle into a bounce. Turn baby around so that she is facing you. Take her hands in yours or hold her around her rib cage.

- Gently bounce the baby on your thighs as you sing or speak the rhyme. Older children might like to slide down your legs on the descending "la" refrain. Babies can gently recline with their head supported by your hand.

- Babies who enjoy being tickled will like it if your fingers walk down their arm from shoulder to wrist on the descending "la" passage. Tickle your baby's hand and tummy when you get to the last note.

DADDY

Place thumb of *open fingers* on forehead, then move hand forward.

Child may tap or point to her forehead.

GAMES TO PLAY

The Royal Treatment

Materials: paper crown

Vocabulary Practice: MOMMY, DADDY, MORE, MUSIC

Other Benefits: imaginative play

Directions: Give your baby the "royal treatment." Make a crown for your child or procure one from your local Burger King™.

Place the crown on the head of your "queen" or "king" as you perform this wiggle. Ask your baby if she is MOMMY'S or DADDY'S queen. Be prepared to serve as her court jester and provide MORE MUSIC.

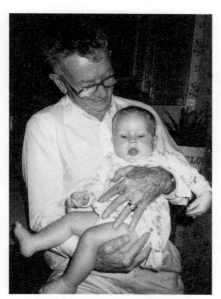

The "Baby King" requires his grandfather do his bidding as well.

Baby's Fun Feast

Materials: trading card plastic protector sheet, pictures of family members

Vocabulary Practice: MOMMY, DADDY, MUSIC

Other Benefits: use of pictures to create meaning

Directions: Insert photographs of MOMMY, DADDY, sister, brother and baby in the pockets of a trading card plastic protector sheet. Now you have a fun "baby placemat" to use to practice this song.

As you sing and sign the song, point to each family member's photograph. The picture mat is also a great diversion for babies as you prepare their meal. Place it on their high chair tray and sing as you dish up dinner. Baby can "read" her MUSIC while you are singing and preparing her food.

Ten out of ten babies surveyed love to look
at photographs of their families.

Ziploc™ Book

Materials: 4-5 Ziploc™ sandwich bags, construction paper, pictures from magazines or coloring books, or photographs, markers, glue, needle and thread, scissors, cloth tape (we used colored electrician's tape over staples)

Vocabulary Practice: MOMMY, DADDY

Other Benefits: book handling and engagement, use of pictures to create meaning

Directions: To create this special book:

1. Cut a piece of construction paper to fit inside each bag, about 3/4 inch shorter and narrower than the bag.

2. Glue a picture or photograph to each page or draw your own.

3. Slip each page into a bag, with the open end of the bag at the right. Zip the bag closed.

4. Sew the unopened ends of two bags together securely with needle and thread, or staple together. Now you have a spread consisting of two pages.

5. Cover the sewn or stapled side with cloth tape.

6. Continue with other pages. If you use a sewing machine, you can easily sew across the edge of 4-5 stacked bags at the same time.

Start with pictures of MOMMY and DADDY in the book. Ask your child to touch the person you request. Change the pictures periodically as your child's vocabulary grows, and ask him to touch or tell you the names of the people and things he sees.

Mommy/Daddy Paper Plate Mask

Materials: two paper plates, tongue depressor, newspaper, stapler, tape, pictures of mommy and daddy (optional: clear contact paper)

Vocabulary Practice: MOMMY, DADDY

Other Benefits: problem solving, grasp and hold movements

Directions: Tape a tongue depressor "lollipop style" between two paper plates. Stuff the space between the paper plates with newspaper to prevent collapse. Staple the plates together, and cover the staples with tape. Affix a different picture on each side of the plates, such as mommy and daddy. You can attach the pictures with clear contact paper to make the toy "drool-proof."

Ask your child if he would like to play with the MOMMY-DADDY TOY. Show him one side and ask him to touch DADDY. Repeat for MOMMY. After he has mastered this game, allow him to hold the toy and ask him, "Is that MOMMY or DADDY?" while pointing to one of the pictures.

BOOKS TO READ

Apperley, Dawn. *Dad Mine!* New York: Little Brown and Company, 2003.

Bauer, Marion Dane. *My Mother Is Mine.* New York: Simon & Schuster, 2004.

Eastman, P. D. *Are You My Mother?* New York: Random House Books for Young Readers, 1960.

Gutman, Anne and George Hallensleben. *Daddy Kisses.* New York: Chronicle Books LLC, 2003.

Katz, Karen. *Daddy and Me.* New York: Little Simon, 2003.

——. *Where Is Baby's Mommy?* New York: Little Simon, 2001.

Marzollo, Jean. *Mama Mama/Papa Papa.* New York: HarperCollins, 2002.

Mayhew, James. *Who Wants a Dragon?* London: Orchard Books, 2004.

Numeroff, Laura. *What Daddies Do Best.* New York: Little Simon, 1998.

——. *What Mommies Do Best.* New York: Little Simon, 1998.

Price, Matthew. *My Daddy.* New York: Knopf Book for Young Readers. 1986.

——. *My Mommy.* New York: Gingham Dog Press, 2003.

Williams, Vera B. *Lucky Song.* New York: Greenwillow Books, 1997.

A SIGN OF SUCCESS
Brainy Babies

Babies come pre-wired. Their brains are covered with billions of neural fibers ready and waiting for stimulation in the form of interesting and appropriate sensory experiences. Never was the phrase "use it or lose it" more fitting. The neocortex is the part of the brain that controls thinking – including reasoning, language and problem solving – and it can be physiologically altered through experience and learning.

Howard Gardner, author of *Frames of Mind* (1993), wrote "in human beings, the density of synapses increases sharply during the first months of life, reaches a maximum at the ages of one to two, declines between the ages of two and sixteen, and remains relatively constant until the age of 72" (pp. 44-45). Birth to three years of age is an important time for the development of motor, music and communication skills, as well as social attachment. *Baby Sing & Sign*™ activities incorporate movement, language and music and provide a balance of novel and familiar ideas to stimulate the baby's developing brain.

Think of your infant's brain as a Chia Pet™. If well tended, this plant will sprout lots of green grass similar to the picture on the packaging. Similarly, infants must be given opportunities to focus on interesting activities and try to figure out their meaning in order for their "green grass" to grow and flourish. Nerve cells that are not stimulated are systematically pruned from birth to around age ten. This pruning is most pronounced in early childhood.

Involvement with music has numerous "brain benefits" for babies and toddlers.

Parents and caregivers can support their baby's rapidly developing thinking skills by providing an assortment of engaging activities during baby's first years of life. Baby's neurological growth is enhanced by involving all of the senses. His brain is a sensory processor, which makes it possible for him to make sense of the external world. The benefits of rich and interesting activities with language and music are maximized when babies experience them in an integrated fashion. That is why "sensory practice" and play-rich environments are beneficial in early childhood. Music and sign language require babies to simultaneously look, listen and move – perfect practice for integrating sensory experiences.

In his book, *Nurturing Your Child with Music* (1999), John Ortiz asserts that early music experiences teach babies to focus their listening skills, and to detect changes in melody, harmony and rhythm. They understand that the voice can be a musical instrument and begin to sharpen their musical memory skills. Hearing a variety of vocal qualities also helps the child to interpret a person's emotional state – such as happy, sad or anxious.

Other "brain-friendly" techniques for helping babies think include:

- Immersing baby in interesting, multi-sensory learning experiences during the course of your daily routine together;

- Creating learning opportunities that provide a balance of novelty and familiarity so that the child is excited but not overwhelmed or bored by the task;

- Allowing baby to problem-solve by actively participating in his learning with a variety of hands-on play materials, games and songs;

- Giving many opportunities to practice new skills so that baby begins to understand there is an order and meaningful pattern to all the information he initially perceives as random experiences;

Baby Sing & Sign™ *activities incorporate movement, language and music and provide a balance of novel and familiar ideas to stimulate the baby's developing brain.*

- Understanding that all learning is emotional and baby's frustration simply means he is developing persistence and passion for problem solving.

Robert J. Shiller said, "the ability to focus attention on important things is a defining characteristic of intelligence" (p. 164). This wisdom applies to parent and caregiver as well as baby. What could be more important than our relationship with the children we love and our interest in setting them on the path to lifelong learning and discovery?

Gardner, Howard. *Frames of Mind.* New York: Basic Books, 1993.

Ortiz, John. *Nurturing Your Child with Music.* Hillsboro, OR: Beyond Words Publishing, Inc., 1999.

Schiller, Robert. *Irrational Exuberance.* New York: Broadway, 2001.

For more information about brain-based learning, check out these books and websites:

Acredolo, Linda and Susan Goodwyn. *Baby Minds: Brain-Building Games Your Baby Will Love*. New York: Bantam Books, 2000.

Brain.org: Practical Classroom Applications of Current Brain Research. http://www.brains.org/.

Brain Connection™. http://www.brainconnection.com/.

EduScapes: A Site for Life-Long Learners of All Ages. http://www.eduscapes.com/.

Gopnik, Alison, Andrew N. Meltzoff and Patricia K. Kuhl. *The Scientist in the Crib: What Early Learning Tells Us About the Mind*. New York: HarperCollins Publishers, 2001.

3
Mommy Go 'Round the Sun

Words To Learn:
CHAIR/SIT, PLAY/TOY

Words To Review:
MOMMY, DADDY

Tips for introducing *Mommy Go 'Round the Sun*

- Ask your child if he would like to PLAY a game with you.

- Place baby on your lap either facing you or with his back leaning against your chest. Bend your knees slightly. Bounce the child to the beat depending upon his preference – some babies like gentle bobbing while others have a more robust taste in their bouncing. *Be sure to provide adequate security for the child by holding him at the waist or hands.*

- Stop the bounce to sign MOMMY, DADDY and CHAIR as the words occur in the song. To free your hands for signing, try sliding the child, facing forward, down your thighs so he is perched securely on your upper legs. Babies who have their backs to you can watch you sign in front of them.

- On the word "boom," you can modify your PLAY by doing any of the following:
  - Give an extra bouncy bounce
  - "Open the trap doors" – open your legs and allow the child to gently land on the floor in between your legs while holding him at the waist or under the arms
  - Lower your straight legs to the floor
  - Introduce an action of your own creation such as a tickle or hug

CHAIR/ SIT

Form *closed two fingers*
palm down with both hands.
Tap one on top of the other, as if
one hand "sits" on the other.

Child may place one *flat hand*
on top of the other.

Mommy go 'round the sun.
Mommy go 'round the moon.
Mommy go 'round the rocking **chair**
Every afternoon. Boom!
Daddy go 'round the sun.
Daddy go 'round the moon.
Daddy go 'round the rocking **chair**
Every afternoon. Boom!

Variations: high chair, baby's chair

"Sally Go 'Round the Sun" from *Sally Go 'Round the Sun* by Edith Fowkes
Copyright © 1969 by the Writers' Union of Canada
Adapted by Anne Meeker Miller

More musical fun with *Mommy Go 'Round the Sun*

- Try making the song an activity that involves moving around. Carry your baby or walk with your child to the beat using a bouncy gait.

- Walk around any chair the child chooses: rocking chair, high chair, daddy's chair, grandma's chair, baby's chair. "Fall down" by sitting on the chair or kneeling to the ground when you get to the "boom."

- Invite siblings, other family members or friends to join you for a "Ring Around the Rosie" version of the song. "All fall down" on "boom."

PLAY/ TOY

Hold hands with thumb and pinky extended and middle three fingers folded. Twist both hands side to side at wrist.

Child may shake *open fingers* with one or two hands.

GAMES TO PLAY

Sally Go in the Car Seat

Materials: high chair or rocking chair, car seat

Vocabulary Practice: CHAIR/SIT, PLAY/TOY

Other Benefits: cooperation, problem solving

Directions: Getting children to cooperate while putting them in their car seats is often a challenge. Here is a playful way to approach this task. Sing "Mommy Go 'Round" as you prepare to put the child into the car seat. Time your singing so that you click the latch shut on "boom." The synchronization of the click and "boom" is fun for baby, and a good experience in predicting auditory events for your baby's developing brain.

Children who are able (and eager!) to climb into their own car seats on their own can play the same game. You may need to speed up or slow down your singing in order to make the click and "boom" come out just right. That can be part of the fun of the game. If your child is very speedy in climbing in and turning around, you will need to sing very quickly. This will appeal to your child's developing sense of humor.

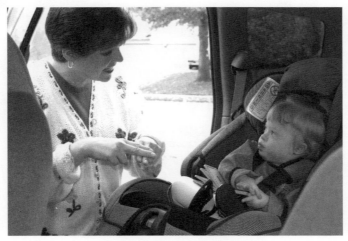

Turn power struggles into PLAY
with a musical car seat game.

Nesting Cans

Materials: tin cans of various sizes, contact paper, cloth tape

Vocabulary Practice: PLAY/TOY, MORE, ALL-DONE

Other Benefits: problem solving, relationships in space, ability to manipulate objects

Directions: Collect several tin cans of various diameters (1-pound coffee can, fruit, soup, tomato paste, etc.). Remove one end of each can. Hammer down any place where metal sticks out on the inside rim. Soak off labels. Cover rims with cloth tape. Cover the rest of the cans with brightly colored contact paper. Your toddler can stack or nest the cans.

Ask your child if she wants to PLAY with the TOY cans. Allow her to stack or nest the cans. If she knocks down a can tower, sign: ALL-DONE? Then ask her if she wants MORE and start the game again.

By playing with toys like the nesting cans, children learn that toys do not have to come from a toy store.

BOOKS TO READ

DK Baby. *Baby Love: Toys That Go*. New York: DK Publishing, 2004.

Ets, Marie Hall. *Play with Me*. New York: Penguin Books, 1999.

Freeman, Don. *Corduroy's Toys*. New York: Viking Press, 1985.

James, Betsy. *My Chair*. New York: Arthur A. Levine, 2004.

Kirk, David. *Miss Spider's Tea Party*. New York: Callaway & Kirk Company LLC, 1997.

Shannon, Terry Miller and Lee Calderon. *Tub Toys*. Berkeley, CA: Tricycle Press, 2002.

Wardlaw, Lee and Russell Benfanti. *The Chair Where Bear Sits*. New York: Winslow Press, 2001.

Wells, Rosemary. *Max's Toys*. New York: Viking Books, 2004.

A SIGN OF SUCCESS

Music and Signing Can Be a Calming Influence for Motor Babies on the Move

Inchworm, inchworm
Measuring the marigolds
Seems to me you'd stop and see
How beautiful they are.

– LYRICS BY FRANK LOESSER
(Featured in the movie *Hans Christian Andersen*)

Have you ever noticed how some babies never stop moving? They are busy, busy, busy people all day long. If you have a busy motor baby in your home, the thought of him slowing down long enough to absorb the signs you want to teach him may appear hopelessly optimistic.

Sarah's two-year-old son, Eric, was a busy motor baby. Calling him active "but not out of control," Sarah wasn't sure what to expect when they first joined a *Baby Sing & Sign*™ class when Eric was ten months old.

"He actually loved it," Sarah explained. "I felt it was a good experience for him." Eric was a crawler constantly on the go, but his mother found he was still tuning in to what was happening around him. "Once the singing started, he would crawl right back," she said. "He was mesmerized by the music."

Music can be an effective way to bring busy motor babies back to a span of attention. Many studies have demonstrated the profound effect music can have on the intelligence and behavior of babies. The intensity of attention to sensory stimuli such as music varies greatly from child to child. Some children respond better to familiar and repeated routines or experiences. Other children more readily focus attention on what's new and different in their world.

Some children respond better to familiar and repeated routines or experiences. Other children more readily focus attention on what's new and different in their world.

"Babies come into the world prepared to enjoy what is novel as well as what is familiar. They pay more focused and intense attention to new stimuli, especially those coming from the human world," wrote Lois Barclay Murphy, Ph.D., and Rachel Moon, M.D. One way to coax attention from your busy motor baby is to continually bring him new and exciting discoveries. The descriptions of the added benefits of the handmade toys and games throughout this book may prove helpful in providing the new stimuli necessary to keep your child focused on learning the signs.

Though boys tend to fall into that busy motor baby category more often than girls, there are many very busy baby girls in the world today, too. Heather participated with her daughter, Taylor, in a *Baby Sing & Sign*™ class just before Taylor's first birthday. Heather describes her daughter as someone who enjoys fully immersing herself in the sensory experiences presented to her.

"She wants to feel it, touch it, experience it with you," Heather explained. "She's curious." Taylor enjoyed the class and was especially enthralled by the class leader's guitar and the silliness that often spontaneously broke out.

Taylor took to signing words well, regularly using PLEASE, MORE, EAT, DRINK, DOG, CAT and FISH. Taylor's parents coped with her tendency to be busily preoccupied by always taking their cues from her when it came to practicing the signs. "When we're at home, I take my cues from her. We do as much as she wants to do," Heather said. Even though she was speaking two-word sentences by eighteen months of age, Taylor continues using her signs. "Sometimes when she gets frustrated or she can't get her point across, she'll resort to signing," Heather said.

Mom and Lucy are making music on the move!

Logan is twenty-two months old and his mother's fourth and last child. Lyn was already well versed in American Sign Language and had taught her older children to sign on her own. Lyn saw the *Baby Sing & Sign*™ class as a way to indulge Logan with some special "just Mommy and me" time as well as offering her a final chance to do something fun with a baby.

"The class looked fun and a good follow-up to what I had already done," Lyn explained. Logan enjoyed the chance to have some interactive fun with all the homemade toys and activities and he really liked the class leader, seeking out and engaging her frequently during the class. At home, Logan's older siblings helped him with his signs and, according to Lyn, getting attention from them became "total positive reinforcement" for what was being taught in class. Logan indicates how much he wants what he's asking for by how emphatically he signs. "He signs with great passion when he really wants something," his mother noted.

According to Murphy and Moon, babies learn about the world either through active exploration or quiet observation. Busy motor babies earn that title because they are the active explorers. And though it may require some extra effort to hold their attention, the benefits of better communication between parent and child make such efforts extremely worthwhile.

Murphy, Lois Barclay, Ph.D., and Rachel Moon, M.D. "Babies and Their Senses." *Zero to Three.* http://www.zerotothree.org/play/.

4
Doggie, Doggie

Words To Learn:
DOG, CAT, BALL

Words To Review:
TOY

Tips for introducing *Doggie, Doggie*

- This song has a very simple tune. Only three pitches are used in the melody. The descending pattern is the essence of this song, which children sing naturally all over the world. The simplicity and repetition of the song enhance the opportunity to practice baby sign.

- Place your child on your lap facing you or with her back to your chest. Sing the song using a moderate tempo, and sign DOG, BALL, CAT and TOY as they occur in the lyrics.

DOG

Pat your side several times
as if calling a dog.

CAT

Draw pinched thumb and pointer
away from cheek, representing
the cat's whiskers.

Doggie, Doggie, who has your **ball**?
Doggie, Doggie, who has your **ball**?
Doggie, Doggie, who has your **ball**?
Doggie, Doggie, who has your **ball**?

Kitty **cat**, Kitty **cat**,
Who has your **toy**?
[Your child's name],
Who has your **book**?

By Anne Meeker Miller

47

More musical fun with *Doggie, Doggie*

Items needed: small ball, toy, medium-sized stuffed toy dog and cat

- Find a small BALL and TOY such as a rattle that baby can hold comfortably in her hand. You will also need a DOG and CAT stuffed animal large enough to cover the small BALL and TOY.

- Hide the ball under the stuffed DOG. Sing the song and pantomime the question, "Who has your BALL?" by raising your eyebrows and looking around for the BALL.

- See if the child will get the BALL from beneath the DOG. If the child does not initiate this action, help her find the BALL by lifting the stuffed DOG.

Opportunities for focused listening and looking are great for developing a child's attention span.

- Ask if the child would like to repeat the game by signing MORE. Play the game again, but now hide the TOY beneath the stuffed CAT.

BALL

Bring hands together to form shape of ball with *open fingers*.

Child may clap hands in up-and-down direction.

GAMES TO PLAY

Time for a Sock Puppet Pet!

Materials: sock, felt scraps, pipe cleaners or garbage bag twist ties, markers, craft glue (or glue gun if available); for a puppet with an opening mouth, you will also need a piece of lightweight cardboard and needle and thread.

Vocabulary Practice: DOG, CAT, BALL, TOY

Other Benefits: receptive language, introduction of two-sign phrases

Directions: Cut felt scraps in the shapes of the eyes, nose and ears of a cat and dog as shown in the photograph. Cut pipe cleaners or garbage bag twist ties for the cat's whiskers. You can also add felt spots to the dog. Put your hand into the sock so that your fingers and thumb are in the toe to determine the best placement for the various pieces. Glue or sew the pieces into place.

You can also make the pet's mouth open by following these steps (see picture on right):

1. Cut a slit in the sock.

2. Cut an oval measuring 3 by 5 inches out of cardboard.

3. Using this cardboard oval as a pattern, cut a piece of felt approximately one-half inch larger.

4. Glue the cardboard to the felt oval, and fold both in half the short way.

5. Turn the sock inside out.

6. Put the folded oval into your sock by placing right sides together, with the felt side of the oval against the outside cut edge of the sock.

7. Stitch the felt piece into the sock using a running stitch.

8. Turn the puppet inside out; he is ready for play.

9. Glue a felt tongue into the mouth along the fold inside the mouth.

You are ready to play! Start with only the DOG puppet. Give your child the small BALL and TOY. Sing the song and finish by saying and signing: Give DOGGIE the BALL. See if the child will give the ball to the DOG puppet. Now play the game singing the CAT verse. Sing and sign: Give CAT the TOY. If your child enjoys the game after many repetitions, she may want to play when you have both puppets on your hands. Most toddlers can differentiate between CAT and DOG and provide the item requested.

The Truth about DOGS and CATS

Signs must have meaning for children if they are to use them in expressive communication with you. If you have a real, live version of a DOG or CAT, these signs will most likely be among the first you will observe your child use in her sign language conversation with you. Do not be offended if CAT and DOG appear long before MOMMY and DADDY.

Please do not use a live dog or cat in any of the games presented here. The same wonderful manual dexterity your child will demonstrate in communicating through gesture can be an irritant for pets – especially when those little fingers end up too close to the animal's ears or eyes.

DOG will likely be one of your child's first signs
if you own (and love) one.

BOOKS TO READ

Boynton, Sandra. *Doggies: A Counting and Barking Book.* New York: Little Simon, 1995.

Carle, Eric. *Have You Seen My Cat?* New York: Aladdin Library, 1997.

Day, Alexandra. *Good Dog, Carl.* New York: Little Simon, 1986.

Eastman, P. D. *Go, Dog, Go!* New York: Random House Books for Young Readers, 1997.

Feiffer, Jules. *Bark, George.* New York: HarperCollins Publishers, 1999.

Henkes, Kevin. *Kitten's First Full Moon.* New York: Greenwillow Books, 2004.

Miller, Virginia. *Where Is Little Black Kitten?* New York: Candlewick Press, 2002.

Wells, Rosemary. *Bingo.* New York: Scholastic Inc., 1999.

A SIGN OF SUCCESS

Patience Is a Virtue (and a Necessity) with *Baby Sing & Sign™*

Every really new idea looks crazy at first.

– ALFRED NORTH WHITEHEAD (1861-1947)

Melinda began taking her daughter, Hannah, to *Baby Sing & Sign™* class when she was six months old. Gung ho about the concept and the class, Melinda was faithful in consistently doing the signs to Hannah and playing the music CD every day. She also taught the rest of the family how to sign for Hannah. When Hannah reached ten months and still showed no inclination to sign back, Melinda got discouraged. Burned out and admittedly tired of doing it, she discontinued signing with the exception of two words: MORE and ALL-DONE.

Several weeks later, Melinda was bathing Hannah in the tub while her daughter played with tub toys. All of a sudden, much to Melinda's amazement and joy, Hannah signed the word FISH while reaching for a plastic fish. "You cannot imagine how excited we were," she said. At twelve months, with Melinda enthusiastic about signing again, Hannah started using the signs for MORE and ALL-DONE. She then rapidly progressed to about ten more signs.

They say patience is a virtue, but it's hard to stay virtuous when you are the parent of an infant or toddler. Busy, hectic lives can interfere, and in a world where instant gratification has become the norm, it can be difficult to "stay the course."

Repetition is essential for baby to learn sign language.

Cathy was another mother who was excited by the prospect of teaching her daughter to sign. They enrolled in *Baby Sing & Sign™* class when Heather was seven months old. The music was an immediate hit but months and months went by with Heather doing no signing at all. Cathy eventually lost interest and only continued to do a few signs on a regular basis, mostly during mealtime.

At fourteen months, Heather did her first sign, MORE. She had been drinking a cup of water and had run out. Her mother signed and asked if she wanted more. The toddler watched her mom do the sign three times, then looked up at her mother's face and signed MORE back. But even as Cathy jumped up quickly to refill the cup with water and return it to her child, Heather showed no interest in drinking. Still, Cathy knew she was demonstrating to Heather that the signs they were practicing had meaning.

They say patience is its own reward, but for most parents the reward comes with the realization that all their efforts have "paid off" and they can now enjoy engaging in true communication with their child.

Take inspiration from the magnificent being you are hoping to teach. No true accomplishment happens overnight.

When you are feeling discouraged and wondering if your pantomiming will ever pay off, take inspiration from the magnificent being you are hoping to teach. When your baby learned to crawl, how long did he rock back and forth on all fours before he finally went in forward motion? How many weeks did your child have to cruise the furniture before he let go and took his first steps unaided? No true accomplishment happens overnight.

As in the famous joke, "How do you get to Carnegie Hall?" (practice, practice!), it takes patience, patience and more patience to get your little star performer to sign.

5
Roll the Ball

Words To Learn:
WANT, PLEASE, HELP, SORRY

Words To Review:
BALL, DOG, CAT, MOMMY, DADDY

Tips for introducing *Roll the Ball*

- This song is destined to be your child's favorite. (You do not need to tell the child that he is developing important motor as well as language and musical skills while doing it!)

- Sit your child on the floor facing you. Gently roll the BALL to baby, and see if he will push the BALL back to you. Babies are most successful with medium-sized, light BALLS such as an inflatable beach BALL. Toddlers enjoy a variety of BALLS.

- Roll the BALL on the lyric "roll." Sing that word slightly louder, giving it the proper emphasis for an action word. Your child may learn to perform the rolling action on cue when it is his turn to roll the BALL to you. Lean side to side on "Roll the BALL, roll the BALL," and then continue the BALL rolling on the last line of the song. See if your child will imitate your rhythmic leaning. He may move his head or rock from side to side.

- Be sure to give the child plenty of time to respond to the game. If necessary, provide a verbal prompt such as "your turn" or "roll the BALL to MOMMY!" Make sure to sing "roll" at the exact moment the child pushes the BALL.

WANT

Pull *open fingers* toward body one time with palms up and fingertips slightly curved, as if drawing something desirable toward you.

PLEASE

Rub *closed fingers* on upper chest in circular motion.

I roll the **ball** to **daddy**,
he rolls the **ball** to me.
I roll the **ball** to **daddy**,
he rolls the **ball** to me.
Roll the **ball**, roll the **ball**,
roll the **ball**, roll the **ball**,
I roll the **ball** to **daddy**,
he rolls the **ball** to me.

2. I roll the **ball** to **mommy**
3. I roll the **ball** to **doggie**
4. I roll the **ball** to **kitty cat**

"Roll the Ball" from *The Book of Simple Songs and Circles* by John M. Feierabend
Copyright © 1996 by GIA Publications, Inc., Chicago, Illinois
All rights reserved.
Adapted with permission by Anne Meeker Miller

More musical fun with *Roll the Ball*

Items needed: balls of different dimensions, weights and textures

- This song gives you another opportunity to practice MORE. When time permits, allow baby to repeat the game until it is her idea to be finished and ready for a new game.

- Be sure to use BALLS of different dimensions, weights and textures. Your baby must learn that BALLS come in all shapes and sizes. The ability to apply one label to several specific items is called "generalization."

- Play or sing the song for your child. Hide a ball behind your back, and ask your baby what she WANTS. If she signs BALL, PLAY or MORE, start the "Roll the Ball" game immediately. If she does not sign in response, start playing the "Roll the Ball" game anyway. There is no keeping score in this ballgame!

- Children often begin using the sign PLEASE interchangeably with MORE once it is introduced. It is never too early to introduce manners! Ask your child if she would like to play ball. Sign PLEASE for her and say "tell me PLEASE." You can also help her make the sign and praise her for her good "talking."

- Ask baby if she will HELP you with a BALL game. Ask her to HELP you with other tasks that will appeal to her. Begin to also use the HELP word in situations where she appears frustrated or could use your assistance. Praise her for asking for HELP by "using her words." Allowing your child to choose to ask for HELP goes a long way toward preserving her dignity while giving her the support she needs to master new skills.

HELP

Place *closed fist* on other *flat hand* and lift both, as if "helping" to raise the closed fist.

Child may cover one hand with the other and lift both.

Love Means *Always* Saying You're SORRY

Children do not come with manners and civility already installed. Some assembly on your part is required.

Focusing on manners from the start will help your child begin to master this essential life lesson. Model your best manners in relationships with others as well as with your child. It is important that you convey the *idea* of how we behave toward one another and add the specifics as life experiences present themselves. Modeling good manners is the best way to teach a child to be polite. Start with basic words, such as PLEASE, THANK YOU (introduced in #9) and SORRY, as soon as your child begins to use signed or spoken words to communicate.

Children also need opportunities to practice their manners with children their own age. Schedule play dates so that your youngster can learn to share her space – and stuff – with others. It is important to establish some ground rules for child play. Although toddlers are not developmentally ready to share their favorite toys with others, parents can help direct playmates in taking turns. Parental praise also goes a long way in encouraging "playing nice." Tell your child, "I like the way you let Tommy play with your blocks."

And, of course, there is the time-honored verbal prompt: "What do you say?" with the expectation that your child will learn which word is called for – PLEASE, SORRY or THANK YOU – and ultimately express these words without you near-by. The best of parents find themselves persisting with this prompt long after the toddler years are over. However, the journey in pursuit of good manners will be much smoother if you start early!

SORRY

Rub *closed fist* on upper chest
in circular motion.

GAMES TO PLAY

Having a Ball with Your Baby

Materials: exercise or other large ball

Vocabulary Practice: BALL

Other Benefits: balance, sensory experience

Directions: Perhaps you purchased an exercise ball in an attempt to return your waistline to its trim pre-maternity measurement. Now you can use it to exercise your arm muscles as well with the assistance of your child. *Babies need good head control in order to play this game.* Put the exercise ball in between your legs or kneel and place the ball in front of you. Place your child on top of the ball – holding him around the rib cage or under the arms – and move him in a circular fashion on the lyric "Roll."

The "rolling" movement shifts the fluid in the inner ear, which influences children's sensation of posture and balance. Modify the rolling movement of the song based on your child's age and preference. Some children (and adults) like the feeling of being out of balance while others prefer staying closer to their center.

"When my daughter was six to seven weeks, I would lay her with her tummy on the exercise ball and gently roll her from side to side and forward and back while supporting her back. I did that as a way to incorporate 'tummy time' but also to begin strengthening her neck muscles. We sang while we gently rolled. When she was able to sit up, we switched to gentle upright bouncing. We used it with your 'Roll the Ball' song. It was a big hit at our house!"

– Amy

Hose Balls

Materials: pair of panty hose, fiberfill, scissors and jingle bell

Vocabulary Practice: BALL, PLAY, MOMMY, DADDY

Other Benefits: develop child's ability to reach, grasp, hold and throw

Directions: Cut a section of the leg from a pair of panty hose and knot one end. Turn inside out and fill with fiberfill to the desired size. Knot the other end. You can wrap a jingle bell inside the fiberfill to make a musical ball.

This ball is easy for young children to manipulate because it is soft and therefore simpler to grasp. Ask your child if he wants to PLAY BALL. Direct him to throw the ball to MOMMY or DADDY. Ask him to "tell me with your hands" who has the ball – MOMMY or DADDY?

BOOKS TO READ

Barrett, John E. *Balls! (Elmo's World)* New York: Random House for Young Readers, 2000.

Churchill, Vickie and Charles Fuge. *Sometimes I Like to Curl up in a Ball.* Pittsburg, PA: Sterling Publishers, 2001.

Holtz, Lara, ed. *Look and Explore: Tumble Times.* New York: Dorling Kindersley Publishing Inc., 2002.

Levy, Constance Kling and Hiroe Nakata. *The Story of the Red Rubber Ball.* Orlando, FL: Silver Whistle, 2004.

Lindgren, Barbro. *Sam's Ball.* New York: William Morrow and Company, Inc., 1983.

Buckley, James, Jr. *Baseball ABC.* New York: Dorling Kindersley Publishing Inc., 2001.

Mayer, Mercer. *Play Ball.* New York: McGraw-Hill Children's Publishers, 2001.

Norworth, Jack. *Take Me out to the Ballgame.* New York: Aladdin Library, 1999.

Ross, Thea. *Lucy Wants to Help.* New York: Parklane Publishing, 2003.

Scholastic. *The Wobbly Bobbly Balls.* New York: Scholastic, 2004.

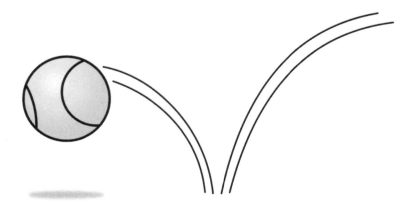

A SIGN OF SUCCESS
Choose to Be Happy

The world is so full of a number of things,
I'm sure we should all be as happy as kings.
But are we?*

The vast majority of expectant parents I know spend hundreds of hours and a great portion of their disposable income preparing the perfect nursery. They fill this special little room with all the things they believe their baby will want and need in the months to come. Family members and friends add more toys and gadgets, often with reassuring recommendations such as "this was Buster's favorite toy" or "when Miguel was little, we couldn't have managed without this fabulous thingamajig."

So many balls to choose from:
red, yellow, green or blue?

And then Baby arrives. For a while, he will agree that for the most part you are doing a splendid job meeting his constant and varied requirements for happiness. In your clairvoyant – albeit sleep-deprived – way you are giving it the "old college try," and your baby thanks you. However, much like the teenager who finds his parents growing more stupid with each passing year (until he grows up and becomes a parent himself), your baby's passage from infancy to toddlerhood will morph from idyllic lovefest to something more closely resembling a food fight. When your child is old enough to throw food at you with passion and purpose, you will know you have truly crossed over.

Babies need caring adults to give them just the right amount of control over the decisions in their lives.

So where did you go wrong? Did you fail to assemble The Right Stuff? Is there a toy or device requisite for good parenting that you somehow overlooked?

The good news is that your toddler's escalating angst is what we call "developmentally appropriate," and has more to do with *how* he gets what he wants than the thing – toy, cracker, power tool – he actually desires. What novice parents rarely understand is that the inner struggle for control begins in infancy, and that what you may consider an abject failure in parenting is in fact an indicator that your child will ultimately be an independent and responsible citizen.

61

However, as with most good things, there is a catch. Babies need caring adults to give them just the right amount of control over the decisions in their lives. Foster Cline, M.D., and Jim Fay, authors of *Parenting with Love and Logic*, suggest that as parents we allow our children to take as much control as possible, "always cutting our kids in on the action."

It is good, right and natural that your child wants to think for himself. The key is to make choices available within a consistent framework of limits. Allowing a young child too much control undermines the benefit of developing independence and creates what is commonly referred to as a "spoiled brat." Trust me when I tell you that you do not want one of those. Psychologist Sylvia B. Rimm, Ph.D., cautions that it is far easier to allow more choices as the child grows older than to take away choices that the child has already enjoyed.

What are some decisions that a toddler can make? Here are a few suggestions:

- Green beans or carrots?
- Blocks or puzzle?
- *Good Night Moon* or *The Runaway Bunny* book?
- "Doggie, Doggie" or "Mommy Go 'Round the Sun" song?

One of the wonders of sign language is that it enables pre-verbal children to express their wants and needs and then make the choices that satisfy their quest for autonomy and control. Make sure you allow your child to utilize his emerging ability to communicate by giving him appropriate opportunities to decide what will happen next.

---

*I remember this line from Donald O'Connor's wonderful performance of the song "Make 'Em Laugh" in the movie *Singing in the Rain*, but I believe Robert Louis Stevenson is the original author. I have found watching this scene with a child is a great remedy for colicky babies and grumpy toddlers. I find it hilarious, and I have the same sense of humor as most of the babies and toddlers I know.

Cline, Foster, M.D., and Jim Fay. *Parenting with Love and Logic*. Colorado Springs, CO: Pinon Press, 1990.

Rimm, Sylvia, Ph.D. *How to Parent so Children Will Learn*. Watertown, WI: Apple Publishing, 1990.

6
The Walking Song

Words To Learn:
ALL-DONE, STOP, OUCH/HURT, HOT

Words To Review:
MORE, WANT, PLEASE

Tips for introducing *The Walking Song*

- Depending on the age of your child, you can either hold her or walk with her in this activity. An older child might enjoy you singing while she performs the actions "solo."

- Walk to the beat of the song and stop in an exaggerated fashion on the lyric STOP. If you have a free hand or are very talented, you may be able to sign STOP while carrying your child.

- At the conclusion of the song, sign ALL-DONE and tell the child "good STOP." Ask her if she would like to sing the song again by signing: MORE?

- Repeat for the other actions in the song. If you are carrying the child, your "hop" can consist of shifting your weight from foot to foot, which causes the child to bounce in your arms. Feeling the rhythmic accent of the bounces is great musical stimulation. The same is true for the "run" action. The faster running bounce is great fun!

ALL-DONE

Hold *open fingers* in front of you with palms toward your chest. Flip hands to palms facing out.

Walking, walking, walking, walking.
Walking, walking, now let's **stop**.
Walking, walking, walking, walking.
Walking, walking, now let's **stop**.

2. Hopping
3. Running
4. **Playing** [music or toys]

Sung to the tune of "Sourwood Mountain"
Traditional
Adapted by Anne Meeker Miller

More musical fun with *The Walking Song*

- STOP, ALL-DONE, PLEASE and MORE can be incorporated into most songs. When you finish a song, sign STOP or ALL-DONE. Ask your child if she wants MORE? She can respond with MORE or PLEASE. When you begin to observe the child using single signs to express her wants and needs, you might want to try and introduce two-sign phrases such as MORE-PLEASE or WANT-MORE.

- You can also make a game of interrupting your singing by signing STOP. You can then sign and ask, "MORE?" Wait for the child to sign MORE or prompt her by helping her sign the word. Tell her, "Good signing MORE!" Then continue singing or playing the music CD. Use the same technique with other signs, such as PLEASE and WANT.

- Try singing the song without the musical recording so you can make the STOP intervals longer and sillier.

- Play "Follow the Leader" at home, at the park or out on a walk while singing the song. Older children will want to take a turn as leader.

- Make up new verses for daily activities such as eating, washing, playing or putting away toys.

STOP

Move little-finger side of one hand
abruptly onto *open palm* of other
hand in a single chopping motion.

Safe Signs

Hannah and her mother spend time together every day walking to the mailbox and singing "The Walking Song." Hannah anticipates the STOP direction in the song by stopping slightly before her mother sings the STOP lyric. Several months after they had started this ritual, Hannah and her mother were shopping at a crowded mall. The little girl managed to get away from her mother and continued running away. As she glanced over her shoulder, she saw her mother sign STOP and immediately halted. This gave her mother the time she needed to catch up to Hannah and retrieve her safely. Signing can be a powerful tool for communicating what is essential to keep your child out of harm's way.

Signing can also help your child communicate pain or discomfort. If you sense your child has injured himself or is not feeling well, sign HURT and ask him where he HURTS. Touch various parts of his body and ask him, "use your fingers" to tell where it HURTS.

Another sign that is helpful for avoiding injury is HOT. This may be used in reference to fire, stoves, radiators or cooked foods. Bobby uses his HOT sign to ask whether a food is too hot to eat every time he is given a dish of FOOD. Although it can be comical to observe him sign HOT with an inquiring look on his face when he is given a dish of ice cream, his caution is appreciated and acknowledged by his parents.

OUCH/ HURT

Both pointers move toward center of body at location of pain.

Child may move fists toward center or point with one hand to location of pain.

HOT

Open fingers of one hand touch chin and then quickly flick out to show that the food is too hot to eat. Can be paired with an "H" sound or blowing.

GAMES TO PLAY

Sound Toys

Materials: empty containers (Tic Tac™ box, film canister, plastic Easter eggs), dried rice, popcorn kernels, electrical tape

Vocabulary Practice: MUSIC, STOP

Other Benefits: reach, grasp and hold movements, listening skills, eye-hand coordination

Directions: Make a variety of sound toys for children to handle and listen to. Try an empty Tic Tac™ box, a 35 mm film canister, a candy bon-bon tin or plastic Easter eggs with dried rice or popcorn kernels inside. Be certain the lids are taped on securely to keep tops and contents out of the child's mouth. Electrical tape can be purchased in primary colors from your local hardware store, and is good for securing your sound toy closures.

These sound toys are great accompaniments to the "playing" verse of "The Walking Song." Sing along with your child and see if she will STOP as directed. Children can improvise their own accompaniment to any tune they choose.

Baby's Kitchen Band

Materials: pots and pans, kitchen utensils

Vocabulary: PLAY, STOP, MUSIC

Other Benefits: reach and grasp movements, eye-hand coordination

Directions: Introduce your child to the joy of playing pots and pans in the kitchen. Use kitchen items with a variety of surfaces such as metal and wood to experience different sound qualities. *Be sure that you are close at hand to monitor your child's safety.* Have your child move her hands to shorten the length of the wooden spoon or spatula used as drum sticks. This will help prevent her from inadvertently whacking herself. Tell the child that you like to listen to her make MUSIC.

After the child has had an opportunity to explore, you can structure sign practice by singing the PLAYING verse of "The Walking Song." Gently place your hands over your child's when you sing STOP, thus preventing her from playing the kitchen MUSIC. Alter the duration of your STOP intervals from just a few to several seconds. Observe carefully how your child tolerates these little episodes of frustration. Does she learn to anticipate where STOP occurs in the song?

Gilli PLAYS the pots and pans
with great enthusiasm!

69

BOOKS TO READ

Crews, Nina. *One Hot Summer Day*. New York: Greenwillow, 1995.

Dodd, Emma. *Hot Dog, Cool Cat: A Crazy Criss-Cross Book of Animal Opposites*. New York: Dutton Books, 2003.

Eastman, P. D. *Red, Stop! Green, Go!* New York: Random House for Young Readers, 2004.

Ellis, Sarah and Ruth Ohi. *Next Stop*. Allston, MA: Fitzhenry and Whiteside Limited, 2000.

Gomi, Taro. *Bus Stops*. San Francisco: Chronicle Books LLC, 1999.

Guthrie, Arlo. *Mooses Come Walking*. San Francisco: Chronicle Books LLC, 1995.

Hubbell, Patricia. *Pots and Pans*. New York: HarperCollins Publishers, 1998.

Katz, Karen. *Excuse Me! A Little Book of Manners*. New York: Grosset & Dunlap, 2002.

Rathman, Peggy. *The Day the Babies Crawled Away*. New York: G. P. Putnam's Sons, 2003.

Szekeres, Cyndy. *Toby's Please and Thank You*. New York: Little Simon, 2001.

Tulip, Jenny. *If You're Happy and You Know It!* Reisterstown, MD: Flying Frog Publishing, Inc., 2000.

Williams, Sue. 1989. *I Went Walking*. New York: Harcourt Brace and Company, 1989.

A SIGN OF SUCCESS
Caregivers and *Baby Sing & Sign*™

It takes a village to raise a child.
– OLD AFRICAN PROVERB

From the moment a baby awakens in the morning until she drifts off to sleep for the last time at night, she is under the watchful eye of a caregiver.

That caregiver is often a parent, but in a society where more and more families have two breadwinners, many babies spend at least a portion of their day in the care of a non-family member. Whether the caregiver is a nanny who comes into your home for one-on-one care; an off-site, in-home daycare provider; or professionals employed by a commercial daycare facility – at the end of the day, your child will have spent most of that day being influenced and guided by others.

In the best of circumstances, a child's caregivers and parents share the same values and work together as a team to ensure consistency in the child's care and upbringing. Communication is as important between parent and caregiver as it is between parent and child, as well as between caregiver and child. Therefore, babies who are being taught sign language benefit most when both parents and caregivers participate.

Margaret shares signs, songs and snuggles with the child she cares for.

Megan is a preschool teacher working at a child and family development center on an urban college campus. Megan uses *Baby Sing & Sign*™'s companion CD during daily group time not only to facilitate the teaching of the signs but also because her charges love the music in and of itself.

She has started teaching her infants and toddlers signs that deal with food and mealtime, such as MORE, WATER and ALL-DONE. "The kids are really happy when they sign MORE and WATER and – bam! – their needs are met," Megan said. "Even the kids who aren't signing yet are beginning to know what it means."

Her center employs advanced technology to document the daily activities of each child. Parents are informed by emails of what new things their child has learned. If a child starts making a sign, it is noted on the daily email. That way parents can ask about the sign the next time they are in the classroom and can choose to reinforce it by demonstrating the same sign at home.

Danielle is a former teacher who for two years has operated an in-home daycare for six children, including two of her own. She has taught the children sign language and has found it helpful in easing children's frustration. In addition to the meal-centered words MORE, ALL-DONE, DRINK and EAT, Danielle has trained her charges to use I'm SORRY and THANK YOU to one another as well as to her.

Babies who are being taught sign language benefit most when both parents and caregivers participate.

"They're very good about signing I'm SORRY to each other," she said. "The kids love the songs and enjoy listening to the CD every day. When a child has mastered a new sign, she will also use it at home, which prompts the parents to inquire the next day about the sign's meaning. "I answer their questions and teach the parents the signs as well," she said. "I have wonderful parents who understand that anything I do with their children has to be done in partnership with them."

While a parent is always a child's first and best teacher, it's important to remember that the village that helps rear her has many fine teachers, too.

7
Where's Baby?

Words To Learn:
EAT/FOOD/SPOON, BOY, GIRL

Words To Review:
SING/MUSIC, PLAY, MOMMY, DADDY,
MORE, DOG, CAT, BALL

Tips for introducing *Where's Baby?*

- Speak the chant very rhythmically. Try for a "sing-song" vocal quality so that you are using the higher part of your vocal range.

- Find a colorful scarf or use a small blanket. Put the blanket across baby's legs. Set baby in your lap with his back toward your chest.

- Rock baby side to side in your lap as you sign MUSIC for the singing line.

- Give baby a bounce or wiggle as you sign PLAY. You can also PLAY with the cloth in baby's lap by flapping or shaking it.

- Gather the edge of the cloth in your hand and bring it to your mouth in a circular motion for "EATING with a spoon."

- Throw the blanket into the air several times when you say, "looking at the moon."

- Place the cloth lightly over the child's head when you say, "My little baby loves to hide from you." Pull it off for "Boo!" Ask your child if he wants MORE. Then start from the top!

EAT/FOOD/SPOON

Place *gathered fingertips* to lips.

74

One little baby **boy [girl]**
Singing through the day.
Two little baby **boys [girls]**
How they love to **play**!
Three little baby **boys [girls]**
Eating with a **spoon**.
Four little baby **boys [girls]**
Looking at the moon.
My little baby **boy**
Loves to hide from you.
Cover up my baby
'Til **mommy [daddy]** says Boo!

By Anne Meeker Miller

More musical fun with *Where's Baby?*

Items needed: bed covers; set of five dogs, cats or balls – can be pictures or small toys

- Let your child cover your head with the cloth and pull it off for "Boo."

- Make the chant into a bounce, adding more rhythmic experience for your child.

- Add this chant to your bedtime ritual using the bedcovers for the motions. The imagery is lovely and you even have a moon to "look at" in the poem.

- Gather a set of five DOGS, CATS or BALLS. They can be picture versions, but three-dimensional items are preferable. They do not need to be matching.

Say the words to the "Where's Baby?" verse and change "baby" to the item you are holding, such as "Doggie," "Kittie Cat," or "bouncing ball." Hand one item to your child each time you count, and then perform its sign. Chances are your child will be watching you carefully to see if you will hand him another toy. This experience in one-to-one correspondence is an early math skill. It is also built-in repetition for practicing sign vocabulary!

BOY

Close fingers to thumb at temple, as if taking hold of the imaginary bill of a ball cap.

GIRL

Drag thumb down side of cheek.

76

Baby Buffet

Food signs are among the easiest to teach because we are all interested and highly motivated learners when given the opportunity to get a tasty snack. Here are some food signs good enough to EAT.

APPLE/ APPLESAUCE

Twist knuckle of pointer on cheek.

BANANA

"Peel" pointer with *gathered fingers* of other hand.

CEREAL

Curve both hands with *fingers closed*. Scoop one hand across the other and up to mouth, as if eating cereal from a bowl.

CHEESE

Press palms of hands together and twist, like pressing cheese.

COOKIE

Tap cupped *open fingertips* on other flat hand.

CRACKER

Tap one *closed fist* on elbow of the other arm.

DRINK

Bring *closed fingers* in "C" shape to lips as if holding a cup.

MILK

Repeatedly squeeze one *closed fist* as if milking a cow.

NOODLE/ MACARONI

Outline the shape of macaroni with both pointers and thumbs, starting at center and pulling out to sides.

GAMES TO PLAY

Peek-a-Boo Book

Materials: two-pocket plastic card protector sheet, pictures/drawings of chosen vocabulary words, felt or fabric square, tape

Vocabulary Practice: BOY, GIRL, DOG, CAT, FOOD

Other Benefits: object permanence, problem solving, use of pictures to create meaning

Directions: Draw or cut out pictures of words such as BOY, GIRL or a FOOD item. Slip the pictures into the two pockets of the plastic page. Tape a square piece of felt or fabric along the top edge of each pocket so that it covers the picture. Ask your child to find the item you request by lifting the felt piece, or ask him to tell you the name of the object. Change the pictures periodically to maintain your child's interest in the peek-a-boo game.

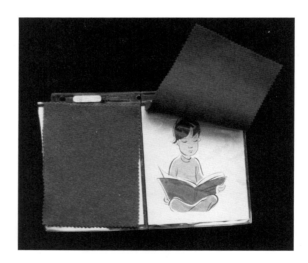

Hide-and-Seek with Signs and Sounds

Materials: colorful scarf or small blanket, small toy cat and dog, musical toy and ball

Vocabulary Practice: TOY, CAT, DOG, BALL

Other Benefits: object permanence, focused listening skills

Directions: Hide small toys or objects underneath a blanket or scarf. Ask the child: "Where's ___?" (TOY, CAT, DOG, BALL) The child can pull the blanket and search for the item you have requested. This is a great way to assess children's "receptive language," or their ability to receive and understand the words you say to them. You can also have the child crawl or walk to the objects to extend the game.

Here is another way to play the game while enhancing your child's awareness of sounds. Hide a musical toy under the cloth and ask the child to "find MUSIC." The toy can be the wind-up variety, a small childproof instrument associated with MUSIC, or a homemade musical instrument. Repeat the game in different locations, and vary the places you hide the toy so that it is challenging and fun.

"Hide-and-Seek" with objects is a great
game for teaching Ella to understand words.

BOOKS TO READ

Ahlberg, Janet and Allan. *Each Peach, Pear, Plum*. London: Penguin Books, 1999.

Barretta, Gene. *On Top of Spaghetti*. Los Angeles: Piggy Toes Press, 2004.

Brett, Jan. *Gingerbread Baby*. New York: Scholastic, 1999.

Brown, Margaret Wise. *Where Have You Been?* New York: HarperCollins Publishers, 2004.

Intrater, Roberta Grobel. *Baby Faces: Eat*. New York: Scholastic, 2002.

Lindgren, Barbro. *Sam's Cookie*. New York: HarperFestival Publishers, 1982.

Moffatt, Judith. *Who Stole the Cookies?* New York: Scholastic Inc., 1996.

Moroney, Christopher. *Sesame Beginnings to Go: Time to Eat*. New York: Random House Books for Young Readers, 2004.

Numeroff, Laura Joffe. *If You Give a Mouse a Cookie*. New York: HarperCollins Publishers, 2004.

Wade, Lee. *The Cheerios Play Book*. New York: Little Simon, 1998.

A SIGN OF SUCCESS

Once Upon a Time:
Creating Traditions for Our Children

There's a place I can see in the best of my memory
Where it'll always be late in July.
When young and unconcerned with the ways of the world,
I was lost in a moment gone by.
So pardon me if I seem old-fashioned
In a world that's changing so fast.
Who would have ever imagined I'd be holding so tight to the past?

– "THE WAYS OF THE WORLD" BY STEVE GILLETTE & REX BENSON*

"Oh no, I've become my mother" is a common – but seldom complimentary – refrain I hear from some of my female friends. In my case, it is my sincere hope that I "become" my mother. She parented me perfectly. There isn't a thing about her I would have changed, and she is everything I hope to emulate in raising my own three children.

My sister, Donna, said it best: "Our mother dedicated herself to making sure our childhood was special." Those of us fortunate enough to have been treasured by our parents as children can be transported back to a family memory in an instant – by a smell, a photo, hearing a familiar song, or returning to a place we once visited with our parents.

Reading "The Night Before Christmas" is one of Kevin's favorite holiday traditions.

The traditions from my past that I recall with great affection were born of necessity rather than design. We camped and canoed because these activities provided affordable family fun. My fondest recollections have something to do with summertime float trips on the Current River in Missouri with my mother, father and sister.

Music was also an important part of my young life. My parents played guitar and sang with us around the campfire. Any spare cash my father had went toward record albums from the latest Broadway shows. By the age of six, I had memorized the lyrics to most of the songs from *The Sound of Music, Guys and Dolls*, and *South Pacific*. The rich musical life of my childhood prepared me well for a lifetime of music as both vocation and avocation.

Carl Caton offers four guiding principles for creating family traditions:

- *The activity needs to be planned and repeated on a regular basis so that your child can look forward to its arrival.* There is nothing sweeter than anticipation. Every year my husband and I take our sons to a Christmas tree farm to select our tree. We take a hayrack ride to the "tree patch," deliberate over at least a dozen possible candidates, finally settle on one, and then chop the tree down ourselves. We must coordinate this outing in early December or – according to our sons – "there will be no trees left." I look forward to this event more than my children do, I think.

- *Make a conscious effort to create traditions.* Most traditions cost nothing but your time, creativity and energy. My parents loved to write poems for us to celebrate special occasions. It wasn't the content of the verse but the thought and effort that went into its creation that made me feel treasured and important.

- *Simple traditions are best.* Life is complicated, and we need to model simplicity and serenity for our children. Take a walk after supper. Read out loud to them in the hammock on a cool afternoon.

- We teachers are fond of *"teachable moments."* These are the special instances when your children are truly in tune with you and open to the nuggets of wisdom or good examples you are eager to share with them. Plan for those moments and make the most of them. Perhaps your family could help serve a meal at a homeless shelter or participate in a charity walk to instill a sense of care and responsibility for others.

Family rituals and special occasions are remembered and cherished in bits and parts – feelings, aromas, silly stories – as evidence of the constancy of the relationship your children have with you.

Most of us know instinctively what we should do to create family traditions. The process evolves as your family grows and you begin to develop lifelong friendships with your children. Your legacy will be the memories you create for them. Family rituals and special occasions are remembered and cherished in bits and parts – feelings, aromas, silly stories – as evidence of the constancy of the relationship your children have with you.

It is totally permissible to borrow fun rituals and traditions from other families. Karen provided me with two that have now become our family's favorites. Thanks to her, my boys often enjoy a "backwards dinner" where we eat dessert before the main course. She also gave me the wonderful idea to award my sons a dime – and effusive praise – for each compliment I receive from others about them. The dime has symbolic rather than monetary value for my boys, and is a nice way of teaching them that their random acts of goodness can sometimes be returned to them in full measure.

Make pancakes on snow days. Take turns sharing one "cheer" and one "challenge" from your day at the dinner table. Sing every commercial jingle you can remember in the car on the way to grandmother's house for Thanksgiving. Make your family pet a cake of his own for his birthday. Set the table with your best dishes on the first day of school. Order Chinese food and watch movies together on Friday nights. Race your child to the top of the stairs at bedtime (and always let her win). Make sure you give your child at least seven hugs a day.

And remind yourself that in a few short years, your children will be passing the traditions you shared with them onto your grandchildren.

---

*I found this song lyric at a folk music website called the Mudcat Café. http://www.mudcat.org/.

Caton, Carl. "The Four Elements of Effective Family Traditions." *People of Faith.* http://www.peopleoffaith.com/family-traditions.htm.

For more ideas about family traditions, check out these books:

Cox, Meg. *The Heart of a Family: Searching America for New Traditions That Fulfill Us.* New York: Random House, 1998.

Ledbetter, J. Otis. *Family Traditions: Practical, Intentional Ways to Strengthen Your Family Identity.* Colorado Springs, CO: Cook Communications, 1998.

MacGregor, Cynthia. *Fun Family Traditions.* New York: Meadowbrook Press, 2000.

Miss Mary Jane

Words To Learn:
CAR, AIRPLANE

Tips for introducing *Miss Mary Jane*

- Place the child on your lap with her back to you. Sign CAR and AIRPLANE in front of the child as you sing the song.

- You can make the song a "bounce" if your child can maintain her balance in your lap while you sign. The child can steady herself by putting her hands on your thighs or outstretched arms.

- There is plenty of space in the lyric for your child's first and middle name ("Miss Anne Marie"). Change the rhythm of the song to best fit the cadence of your child's name.

CAR

Place *closed fists* in front of you
and move them up and down
alternately as if holding on
to a steering wheel.

AIRPLANE

"Fly" *open hand* with ring and
middle fingers folded down
in an upward direction.

Riding in a buggy, Miss Mary Jane,
Miss Mary Jane, Miss Mary Jane,
Riding in a buggy, Miss Mary Jane,
We're a long way from home.

2. Riding in a **car**
3. Riding in a **wagon**
4. Other ideas: **truck, train, airplane**

From *On the Trail of Negro Folk Songs* by Dorothy Scarborough
Copyright © 1925 by Harvard University Press, Cambridge, Massachusetts
This song was provided to Ms. Scarborough by W. F. More, York County, South Carolina.

More musical fun with *Miss Mary Jane*

Items needed: large ball, toy dog or cat, wagon, bike or stroller ("buggy"), laundry basket and towel or blanket

- Substitute anything you can think of for the "buggy" lyric, including nonsensical things such as clouds, camels and carrots.

- You can also incorporate other baby signs and ride a DOG, CAT or BALL. You may have "toy" versions of these items large enough to seat your child on so that the child can have a fun ride.

- "Riding in a Buggy" is the perfect music to travel by. Sing with gusto as you and baby take a trip to the park or through the neighborhood via wagon, bike or buggy. Be sure to synchronize the spring in your step to the beat of the tune. (Try to ignore passersby who stare in wonderment.)

- Laundry baskets make wonderful "buggies," CARS, AIRPLANES, trucks and trains. Place your toddler in a plastic laundry basket and add a folded towel or blanket underneath the "driver" for added stability. Give your child a push or pull around the living room. Make sure to add a sound so your vehicle has an imaginary engine!

Wagons are wonderful "baby buggies."

GAMES TO PLAY

Rice Bin Dig

Materials: plastic bin or other covered container, rice or dried oatmeal, small toys, books and items for scooping and pouring, plastic tablecloth/ shower curtain

Vocabulary Practice: BOOK, BALL, TOY, CAR, AIRPLANE, SPOON

Other Benefits: reach and grasp movements, tactile stimulation, object permanence, pre-math concepts

Directions: Fill a large, covered container with rice or dried oatmeal. Gather small objects such as board BOOKS, BALLS, TOY CARS, AIRPLANES or animals, butter bowls and SPOONS and drop them into the bin.

Allow your child to experience the feel of the grain and practice the fine-motor skills of scooping and pouring. Place the bin on a large plastic tablecloth or shower curtain to make clean-up easier. Ask the child to find the item you request in the bin. You can also ask him to sign the name of the item he finds.

Deirdre enjoys the different "feel" of things.

To ensure success, the requested item in the bin may be placed closest to the child. This is called "errorless learning." As the child is able to locate the requested item, the task can be made more challenging by moving the item farther away or hiding it under the rice.

BOOKS TO READ

We judge how much we love books at our house by the condition of their binding. There are only a few fibers remaining on the binding of our *Cars and Trucks and Things That Go* by Richard Scarry (Random House Children's Books, 1974). Mr. Scarry is a genius at creating engaging and imaginative books for young readers. Each two-page spread of *Things That Go* contains dozens of whimsical wheeled vehicles, including my favorite – the Pickle Car. There is also a small gold bug we called "Gold Buggie" to hunt for on each page.

Repetition is good. You will find wonderful song material for the "Riding in a Buggy" song in the pages of this book. Make the most of your child's developing love of books and music by singing new verses until it is your child's decision to stop the game.

And be sure not to skip any pages!

MORE BOOKS TO READ

Berry, Bob. *Big Red Car*. New York: Grosset & Dunlap Inc., 2003.

Guthrie, Woody. *New Baby Train*. New York: Little Brown & Company, 1999.

Kirk, David. *Miss Spider's New Car*. New York: Scholastic Press, 1999.

Ladybird. *I Like Cars*. New York: Ladybird Books Limited, 1999.

Pallotta, Jerry. *Airplane Alphabet Book*. Watertown, MA: Charlesbridge Publishers, 1997.

Pratt, Pierre. *The Very Busy Life of Olaf and Venus: Car*. New York: Candlewick Press, 2001.

Raffi. *The Wheels on the Bus*. New York: Crown Publishers, 1988.

Sturges, Philemon. *I Love Planes!* New York: HarperCollins Publishers, 2003.

Ziefert, Harriet. *Train Song*. New York: Orchard Books, 2003.

A SIGN OF SUCCESS
Boys and Girls at Play

What are little girls made of?
Sugar and spice and all things nice,
That's what little girls are made of.
What are little boys made of?
Snips and snails and puppy dog tails,
That's what little boys are made of.

– MOTHER GOOSE

The great debate among child development theorists has to do with "nature versus nurture," and whether our biology is more or less important than the opportunities in our environment that allow us to learn and grow. I remember very little from my first undergraduate course in psychology, but do I recall some discussion of "tabula rasa" or blank slate. The belief forwarded by John Locke (1632-1704) was that children begin life with no predisposition for intellect or behavior. Knowledge and character result from experience, thereby gradually filling the blank slate.

This notion fueled my pre-motherhood teaching, giving me reason to believe that all of my students had an equal opportunity to master the concepts and skills I taught. I still believe that all children can learn, but recognize that they benefit most from teaching methods that are customized to fit their unique learning styles and preferences. Some children learn best by listening to instructions, while others prefer to watch or actively participate in order to learn a new skill or concept.

As a proud graduate of "The School of Motherhood," I have learned that boys and girls often learn in distinctly different – and gender-specific – ways.

The same holds true for parenting. The "handbook" you devise to guide your first offspring through childhood is suddenly obsolete when your second baby joins the family. The observations you make about your children the day they are born are often good predictions of the personality characteristics they will exhibit into adulthood. Remember the comments you and your family made to one another as you checked your new little one out? When you made certain the baby had the requisite number of body parts while all marveled at his perfection, you might have used descriptors ranging from "mellow" to "active" or "eager." Are those traits still readily observable in your child today? The "tabula" your baby was issued at birth may not be as blank as Locke would have us believe.

It appears there are some enduring truths about raising girl- and boy-flavored babies as well. I am the mother of three sons, which proves that God has a sense of humor. I was raised with one female sibling, and was ill-prepared for the rigors of being a mother of males. As a proud graduate of "The School of Motherhood," I have learned that boys and girls often learn in distinctly different – and gender-specific – ways.

Parents I've met who are vigilant about providing activities for their children that avoid gender stereotyping share similar stories. It does not seem to matter that you have carefully avoided all toys, games and play activities that could be deemed "boy" or "girl." Your female child will still want to carry a purse. Your male child will want to point whatever he is holding in his hand at someone – often his grandmother – and make violent "pow pow" noises.

Miss Jaylie loves her fancy purse.

Studies investigating male and female biological differences, as well as the influence of experience and culture, usually raise more questions than they answer. While it is generally acknowledged that men and women use different parts of their brains to learn and problem-solve, it remains unclear to what extent environment and opportunity interact with biology in this process.

Michael Gurian, author of *The Wonder of Boys* (1997), finds that boys are more spatial and visual in approaching games and thus require more physical space, whereas girls tend to be more verbal and emotional in their play. Boys often process their feelings through action, which translates to more observable gross-motor activity. Girls tend to be able to maintain interest in objects and fine-motor activity for longer intervals than boys, and are biologically inclined to be able to do several tasks at the same time. Gurian also suggests that girls on average are better at verbal tasks and reading, while boys tend to excel at spatial and analytical tasks such as math.

In his newest book, *Boys and Girls Learn Differently* (2001), Gurian claims there are also gender differences in language development, with females producing more words than males. "We often find girls using words as they learn, and boys often working silently," he wrote (p. 45).

Boys and girls may listen differently as well. Deborah, a primary-school teacher, reported that her male students seemed to listen better when they had something else to do at the same time, such as draw or take a walk (Gabriel, 2001).

Be careful not to jump to conclusions about your child based on research studies that cluster children into groups. Averages and estimates are of little help in inspiring the greatness within one baby boy or girl, as each child differs "wildly" from the next (Gabriel, 2001). The reality is that there are certain activities your child – whether boy or girl – will find inherently more interesting and engaging than others. Children must be engaged in an activity to learn. Learning is good. Ergo, roll with it.

Your boy-child's favorite songs in this collection will probably be "Roll the Ball," "Riding in a Buggy" or any song involving motor skills such as running and running – so clear the "dance floor" and get ready to move! Your girl-child may really like "Doggie, Doggie" or any song involving long, heartfelt conversations with her stuffed animals. Girls will also want to demonstrate their outstanding fine-motor skills, such as putting objects in and taking objects out of something like ... a purse!

Gabriel, Jerry. "The Truth About Boys and Girls." *Brain Connection.* http://www.brainconnection.com/content/.

Gurian, Michael. *Boys and Girls Learn Differently!: A Guide for Teachers and Parents.* San Francisco: Jossey-Bass, A Wiley Company, 2001.

——. *The Wonder of Boys.* New York: Penguin Putnam Inc., 1997.

9
The Little Cat Goes Creeping

Words To Learn:
SLEEP/BED, FISH, THANK YOU

Words To Review:
CAT

Tips for introducing *The Little Cat Goes Creeping*

- Carry your baby as you sing this song. Toddlers can do the walking themselves. Model the motions suggested by the song in an exaggerated fashion.

- Let your movements mimic the music for each verse. For example, the CAT should creep on tiptoe at a moderate tempo. The FISH is a smoother-gliding motion as he swims. The baby SLEEPING is a slower walk with an upper-body rock from side to side.

- Finish the song by lying down on the floor for a nap. You can even lay your child on the couch or floor at the end. Cover the child with a blanket and tell her "night, night!"

- Tell your child THANK YOU for PLAYING the CAT game with you. Ask her if she would like to PLAY some MORE?

SLEEP/BED

Place *flat hand* palm-side up on side of head and tilt head, as if head rests on a pillow.

FISH

Hold one *flat hand*, thumb-side up, with other *flat hand* touching at wrist. Move both hands forward, with front hand fluttering to imitate fish swimming.

The little **cat** goes creeping,
Creeping, creeping
The little **cat** goes creeping
All through the house.

2. The little **fish** goes swimming
3. The little baby's **sleeping**
[Baby can also run, jump, march]

More musical fun with *The Little Cats Go Creeping*

Items needed: basket, objects or pictures representing animal signs (DOG, CAT, FISH) and GIRL and BOY

- Make up verses for DOG, MOMMY and DADDY. Ask your child to show you how she walks. Then think of an action word that matches her motion, and sing a new verse. For example, "The little DOG goes jumping."

- Make a "vocabulary basket" of animals. Put objects representing the signs you are teaching such as beanie animals or pictures in a basket. Have your child take out DOG, CAT and FISH and sing a verse for each. You can also include GIRL and BOY if you have dolls or pictures that can represent children.

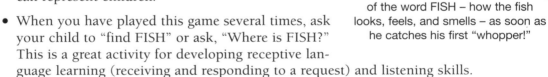

Isaac will learn first-hand the meaning of the word FISH – how the fish looks, feels, and smells – as soon as he catches his first "whopper!"

- When you have played this game several times, ask your child to "find FISH" or ask, "Where is FISH?" This is a great activity for developing receptive language learning (receiving and responding to a request) and listening skills.

- Select two objects and place them on the floor. The items may be positioned at a distance from your child, encouraging him to crawl or walk to the desired object. Ask him to "Get the FISH." A toddler may be able to sign or speak in response to the question, "Which one is FISH?"

- Say the "Where's Baby?" poem (#7) and substitute FISH for BOY or GIRL.

- Add THANK YOU to communication with your child in response to any sign or vocalization he shares with you. This way, you are modeling the good manners you want your child to demonstrate with yourself and others.

THANK YOU

Touch *closed fingers* to lips and then extend them down.

GAMES TO PLAY

Baby Safari

In the words of the immortal artists Marvin Gaye and Tammy Turell, "Ain't Nothin' Like the Real Thing, Baby." Take a field trip to your local petting zoo or farm so that baby can see first-hand how the animals move. Listen carefully to how the animals sound as well. Try and imitate the sounds and see if your child will join in. Call baby's attention to the animals that make no sound at all. Focused listening and awareness of sound and silence are important fundamental music skills for young children.

You have mastered the animals in motion and met them "up close and personal." It is now time to play an animal sound game at home. Point to your ear for SOUND and sign an animal. Ask your child "what SOUND does the CAT make?" Continue the game for all the animal signs you have learned. Play the game with other animals as well.

Trips to the petting zoo provide
multi-sensory experiences for children –
sounds, sights, smells and more.

Goldfish Bowls

Materials: empty yogurt container, scissors, Goldfish™ or other snack cracker or cereal

Vocabulary Practice: FISH, EAT, MOMMY, DADDY

Other Benefits: reach and grasp movements, eye-hand coordination, problem solving

Directions: Place Goldfish™ or other snack crackers in an empty yogurt container. In attempting to get the snack, your child can practice reaching, pouring and grasping. With the lid on, the container can be a shaker to accompany music. Toddlers will enjoy dropping the cracker into the container when a hole is cut in the lid.

Ask your child if he wants to EAT FISHIES. Place the crackers on the high chair tray or table. Ask him to give a FISHIE to MOMMY or DADDY. Give the child a few Cheerios™ along with the Goldfish™ crackers and ask him to find the FISHIE. Ask him what the FISHIE is called.

BOOKS TO READ

Bucchino, John. *Grateful: A Song of Giving Thanks*. New York: HarperCollins Publishers, 2003.

Crum, Shutta and Sylvie Daigneault. *All on a Sleepy Night*. New York: Stoddard Publishing Co. Limited, 2001.

Eagle, Kin. *Rub a Dub Dub*. Dallas, TX: Whispering Coyote Press, 1999.

Ehlert, Lois. *Fish Eyes: A Book You Can Count On*. New York: First Red Wagon Books, 2001.

Ellwand, David. *Ten in the Bed*. Brooklyn, NY: Handprint Books, 2000.

Fox, Mem. *Time for Bed*. New York: Harcourt Brace and Company, 1993.

McLean, Wendy. *Friendly Fish*. North Vancouver, BC: Whitecap Books, 2002.

Scarry, Richard. *Richard Scarry's Please and Thank You Book*. New York: Random House for Young Readers, 1973.

Simon, Mary Manz, Linda Clearwater, and Kathy Couri. *Squirrel Says Thank You (First Virtues for Toddlers)*. Cincinnati, OH: Standard Publishing Company, 2003.

Wood, Audrey and Bruce Wood. *Ten Little Fish*. New York: Blue Sky Press, 2004.

A SIGN OF SUCCESS

Siblings Are a Benefit When Teaching Babies Sign Language

It is with our brothers and sisters that we learn to love, share, negotiate, start and end fights, hurt others, and save face. The basis of healthy (or unhealthy) connections in adulthood is cast during childhood.

– JANE MERSKY LEDER

Going from being the only child to the older sibling has its good days and its bad days. What a huge shock it can be to a youngster when his parents bring home a noisy blob in a blanket and no longer is he the center of the universe.

Amy recalls the day she and her husband brought their new infant son, Gianni, home from the hospital. Her nearly three-year-old daughter, Isabella, looked more than a little alarmed. "When you bring your new baby home, the older kid looks at the baby like 'what is this?' and 'what do I do now?'" Amy said.

Gianni learns to sign EAT from his older sister – and favorite sign language teacher.

Many older siblings will take on one of two roles when a new baby moves in: avid competitor or co-parent. Sometimes it is the age difference that prompts the role, and sometimes it is the personalities of the children involved. Asking the sibling to help teach the new baby to sign is one way to encourage the co-parent role. Now that Gianni is seven months old, Isabella enjoys reinforcing the signs that her mother is teaching by also using them in interaction with her brother.

Isa used sign language before she learned to talk but hadn't used the signs in more than a year. Amy was pleased to discover she only had to show Isa a sign one time for her to pick it right back up again. One day Isa saw Gianni advancing toward one of her books with a gleam in his eye. Rather than yelling or screaming at her baby brother, Isa made the sign for STOP. Her mother was pleased. "It's nice that she made the connection to use the sign instead of carrying on," Amy said. "Isa also signs MILK to Gianni and he will kick his legs in anticipation, just as she did when she was a baby and I would sign MILK to her."

Darcy and David have three daughters, whom they taught to sign. According to Darcy, "the benefits are never-ending." Darcy has found that in making the signing a family affair, there is never a breakdown in communication and the baby's wants and needs can be met even if she is not standing right there. "For example," she said, "Mollie is in the high chair and I am cooking dinner. If she signs MILK and my other two girls see her, then they offer her the milk or they tell me." Darcy believes signing has helped her girls develop a very strong bond with each other by fostering playtime that's not always adult-driven but is instead extended from child to child.

Kelly became interested in signing after the birth of her firstborn, Jack. She obtained books and taught herself and her son to sign. "I started with Jack when he was four months old. He's now three-and-a-half years old and he has great verbal ability that I attribute to signing," she explained. Kelly recalls that Jack particularly used his signs when "he meant business." Now Jack is big brother to eighteen-month-old Ava, with all the duties and responsibilities that entails.

> *Darcy believes signing has helped her girls develop a very strong bond with each other while fostering playtime that's not always adult-driven but extended from child to child.*

"I told Jack he had to help me sign with Ava because Mom was too busy sometimes," Kelly said. "He immediately picked up the signing again." Because Ava is Jack's little shadow, she is prone to emulate what she sees her brother doing – another benefit that siblings bring to *Baby Sing & Sign*™. Ava participated in the *Baby Sing & Sign*™ class when she was six months old. Her mother said her signing peaked when she was ten to thirteen months old. Though now also honing her excellent verbal skills, Ava continues to sign, especially to her cousin, who is six months younger.

Siblings gain confidence when they share with and teach one another, and older children are natural role models for the young ones who follow. Parents can tap in to this natural tendency for the older child to lead, making the learning experience beneficial for all.

10
Bunny Boogie

Words To Learn:
BUNNY

Words To Review:
EAT

Tips for introducing the *Bunny Boogie*

- Place baby on your lap with her back to your chest. Bounce her gently on the words "hop, hop, hop." Sign the word BUNNY as it occurs in the text.

- Babies who enjoy bearing weight on their feet can stand between your bent legs. Support the baby by placing your hands under her arms or on her rib cage. Bounce the baby gently or hold her while she does the bouncing herself. Give the child an extra little lift on the words "hop, hop, hop."

- Your hands will not be free to sign BUNNY. Use the sign at the end of the song in comments such as, "Are you my BUNNY?" or "BUNNY hops!"

- Sign EAT for "Chew your carrot." You can make the gesture to your mouth or your child's mouth, as if you are feeding her the carrot.

BUNNY

Closed fingers form bunny ears and "wiggle" backward at top of head.

Child may wiggle all five fingers with one or both hands, or place both hands by ears.

Hop like a **bunny**, hop, hop, hop
Hop like a **bunny**, hop, hop, hop
Hop like a **bunny**, hop, hop, hop
Hop like a **bunny**, hop, hop, hop

2. Wiggle your ears and hop
3. Wiggle your tail and hop
4. Chew your carrot [**eat**] and hop
5. Hop like a bunny

I said you bunny,
I love you, bunny,
You hippy, hoppy, funny bunny,
Hop, hop, hop – Yeah!

By Anne Meeker Miller

101

More musical fun with the *Bunny Boogie*

Items needed: food pictures cut from magazine or other source, index cards, trading card plastic protector sheet

- Most toddlers enjoy trying to hop on their own while holding your hands. Two adults can help the child hop by each holding a hand and lifting her on "hop, hop, hop."

- Extend the bunny fun while toning your thighs. Hold your child tight and hop with the child on "hop, hop, hop." Many children learn to hop independently with both feet together from around eighteen months to two years of age. This vicarious hop is a good simulation of their own future hopping and will show them that you know how to play!

- *I do not recommend children eating and hopping at the same time.* To use the "Bunny Boogie" to teach FOOD signs, cut pictures of your child's favorite food out of a magazine, mount them on index cards and slip them into the pockets of a trading card plastic protector sheet. Ask your child to point to the food she wishes to sing about by signing: What do you WANT to EAT? Once the child has made her selection, you can sing the song with her food choice: "Chew your CRACKER and hop, hop, hop!" This strategy makes food and hopping a safe, fun game. Your child is also exercising her musical "muscles" as she creates her own composition.

GAMES TO PLAY

Baby's Play Book

Materials: trading card plastic protector sheets for musical instrument, family member and food/hopping game, ribbon, plastic cord or loose-leaf rings (and electrical tape)

Vocabulary Practice: MUSIC, MOMMY, DADDY, EAT

Other Benefits: use of pictures to create meaning, pre-reading skills

Directions: Several suggestions have been made throughout this book for using trading card plastic protector sheets:

- "Clap Your Hands" musical instrument game
- "This Is the Father Wiggle" family member game
- "Hop Like a Bunny" food and hopping game

Children enjoy a "play book" of their own. Here's how to make one. Fasten the pages from the games listed above together with ribbon, plastic cord or loose-leaf rings. *If using the latter, be sure to tape the closed ends of the rings with electrical tape to prevent them from pinching or scratching baby.*

One of the benefits of "expressive language," or the ability to communicate our wants and desires, is the power to make choices. Children love to make decisions about the activities of their daily lives. The "play book" is a way for them to show you the game they want to play with you.

The book is also a wonderful pre-reading activity. It is never too early for children to learn that people and things they desire can be symbolically represented with pictures. The pictures will reinforce the sign language vocabulary you are teaching. Your child may require help manipulating the pages to make her game choice. Be sure to take the pages with you to the grocery store and allow your child to make food choices and add them to your shopping cart. Singing is allowed in most supermarkets.

Isa is in touch with her inner – and outer – BUNNY.

103

BOOKS TO READ

Brown, Margaret Wise. *Bunny's Noisy Book*. New York: Hyperion Books for Children, 2002.

——. *The Runaway Bunny*. New York: Harper & Row Publishers, 1942.

Ga'g, Wanda. *The ABC Bunny*. New York: Putnam and Grosset Group, 1933.

Jeram, Anita. *Bunny My Honey*. Cambridge, MA: Candlewick Press, 1999.

McMullan, Kate. *If You Were My Bunny*. New York: Scholastic Inc., 1996.

Nakamura, Katherine R. *Song of Night: It's Time to Go to Bed*. New York: Scholastic Inc., 2002.

Pfister, Marcus. *Hopper*. Gossau Zurich, Switzerland: North-South Books, 1991.

Walton, Rick. *Bunnies on the Go*. New York: HarperCollins Publishers, 2003.

——. *So Many Bunnies*. New York: HarperFestival Publishers, 1998.

A SIGN OF SUCCESS

The Wonder-Filled World of Whimsy: The Importance of Imagination, Creativity and Humor in the Life of a Child

Imagination is more important than knowledge.
Knowledge is limited.
Imagination encircles the world.

– ALBERT EINSTEIN

My grandfather was a very funny guy.

He took me to an amusement park when I was a preschooler and told me to wait in the car while he went for a pony ride. When I mentioned that I might like to take a pony ride as well, he pretended to be surprised that I would be interested in riding a pony, and then invited me to join him.

The following day, I called him to chat as I often did. During our conversation he told me that he was busy watching my grandmother ride a pony in their living room. I am told that I exclaimed, "Grandpa, I didn't know you had a pony!" And as you would expect, I immediately started pestering my mother to drive me at top speed to grandfather's house. I wanted to see grandma riding that pony for myself. I don't suppose my mother thought that Grandpa's game of pretend was as wonderful as I did that day.

Mine was a charmed upbringing filled with people who made it their mission to teach me the value of whimsy – the capacity for unrestrained imagination in the face of reason and reality. I had a rich variety of experiences and opportunities to pursue activities that interested me. My ideas were valued and incorporated into our daily lives as a family. My artistic, musical and literary creations were admired and shared with others in my circle of significant adults. I felt cherished, and that is the safest of places to start from as you venture out into the world to try new things and explore the possibilities life holds.

A parent or caregiver's ability to laugh and indulge in the unadulterated joy of life with children is a bonding experience like no other.

Imagination, creativity and humor make a great difference in preparing children for a life of joy and adventure. A baby's first smile – the kind you know was caused by amusement and not gas – is reason for celebration, and provides encouragement for parent and caregiver that the child notices you and finds you clever and interesting. Babies' smiles and giggles are truly addictive, prompting most of us to try out our entire repertoire of funny faces and fancy dances to get a reaction. Once we determine what makes our baby smile, we persist in doing it again and again. The favor will be returned when your child begins to entertain you with her antics. No longer will you need to leave your home or turn on a television set for entertainment.

Researcher Carolyn Chaney explored how humor develops in infants and toddlers. She found that once babies can form expectations of what will happen next in their lives, they often laugh or smile when the unexpected occurs. When playing games such as "Hide and Seek" or "Chase," a child delights in the unexpected outcome – how will my playmate find me? The "baby humor" can be heightened when the playmate varies the outcome of the game by finding a new hiding place or altering how long the child must wait to be found.

Laughter is music to the ears of a young child!

Parents and caregivers can help children recognize humor by giving them cues. Exaggerated motions or facial expressions, as well as vocal inflection, help teach children to find the "funny" in a variety of experiences. A verbal prompt such as "are you teasing me?" or "you're a funny bunny" in response to your child's playfulness will remind him of his own potential for humor and joking.

Developing your child's sense of humor will also help you keep yours, which comes in handy as you move through the more treacherous moments of parenthood. A parent or caregiver's ability to laugh and indulge in the unadulterated joy of life with children is a bonding experience like no other, and a wonderful attribute to share.

Laura Murphy, president of Real Families, Inc., shares a great story about the importance of humor in her family. "From the time our kids were babies, they have sensed and participated in the warmth of humor in our household. However, I've never heard it more eloquently put than the way it was described by our ten-year-old son. One night, after a particularly fun dinner time at our house, my son said to me, 'Do you know what I love best about Dad? It's that he can make us laugh so hard that I feel as if I don't know where my next breath is going to come from. It really is the greatest feeling in the world.'"

Once a child learns to play his own "jokes" with pretending games – that his rubber duckie can quack, bananas make funny noses, and daddy will never find him if he hides in a laundry basket – parents and caregivers can begin to nurture his creativity in other ways as well. Karen Miller, child development specialist, suggests that parents encourage children's creativity and imagination by helping them:

- Feel valued
- Learn to combine things
- Explore space and direction through motor movement
- Have opportunities to hold and manipulate objects and materials
- Make a mess
- Enjoy a variety of experiences

In his book, *Playful Parenting*, Lawrence Cohen describes play as "a place of magic and imagination where a child can be fully one's self" (p. 4). A youngster who impersonates a monkey or who sings from the top of the "mountain" as she plays on the swing set in her backyard is honing her skills for innovation and originality. Parents who join in these games can relive play memories from their own childhood and have a lot of fun in the process.

Music can provide wonderful opportunities for imagination and creativity. Marjorie, a veteran music as well as preschool and elementary teacher, believes that rhythm comes first as young children begin to create music. For example, they can pat a playful beat as they sing or tap a tune all their own using their spoon and high chair tray. Sound play and creation of movements to accompany singing are also favorite activities of very young children. Marjorie often asks her youngest students to make up songs using their "show and tell" items for musical inspiration. She writes down the songs for them to keep and share with their families.

Children whose families foster their creativity and imagination incorporate those competencies into their sense of self. Marjorie shared a story about one of her three-year-old students who was hard at work creating an art project with markers, glue and buttons. Marjorie commented, "You are doing such a nice job on your picture."

The little girl replied: "Thank you. I've been an artist all my life."

Get in touch with your inner toddler. Revisit that creative, enthusiastic youngster you were many years ago, and invite her to make a play date with the baby at your house.

Imagine the possibilities!

Chaney, Carolyn. "Young Children's Jokes: A Cognitive Developmental Perspective." Paper presented at the Annual Meeting of the Western States Communication Association (Albuquerque, NM, February 14, 1993).

Cohen, Lawrence J. *Playful Parenting: A Bold New Way to Nurture*. New York: Ballentine Books, 2001.

Miller, Karen. "Caring for the Little Ones: Creative Activities for Infants and Toddlers." *Child Care Information Exchange*, 113 (Jan-Feb 1997), 35-37.

Real Families. www.real-families.com.

Here are some books for parents to read regarding humor, creativity and imagination:

Michelli, Joseph. *Humor Play & Laughter: Stress-Proofing Life with Your Kids*. Golden, CO: The Love and Logic Press, 1998.

Schank, Roger. *Coloring Outside the Lines: Raising a Smarter Kid by Breaking All the Rules*. New York: HarperCollins Publishers, 2000.

11

Charlie Over the Water

Words To Learn:
WATER

Words To Review:
FISH, MOMMY, DADDY

Tips for introducing *Charlie Over the Water*

- This song should be sung with the proper enthusiasm due a wonderful old sea chantey. Sing the lyrics with an accented quality, as if you are rowing a boat to the beat of the tune.

- Change "Charlie" to your child's name. You can also substitute MOMMY and DADDY.

- Sign WATER as it occurs in the song.

WATER

Tap pointer of *open fingers* on the middle of your chin several times.

Child may tap chin with all four fingers or *gathered fingertips*.

Charlie over the **water**,
Charlie over the sea,
Charlie catch a **fishie**,
Can't catch me!

Substitute your child's name,
mommy or **daddy**

Traditional
Adapted by Anne Meeker Miller

More musical fun with *Charlie Over the Water*

Items needed: bathtub or swimming pool, water toys, blanket (preferably blue)

- Try playing a marching "follow the leader" game as you sing. Make your march go high and low by standing on your tip-toes and bending your knees. You can even add a jump on your child's name.

- Try another game called "Catch Charlie." Sing the song through and when you get to "can't catch me," start running and see if your child will follow. When the child "catches" you, he gets to be the leader and run next.

- Sing your Charlie song in the WATER during bathtime or on a trip to the swimming pool. Add toys and mix thoroughly with PLAY!

- Your toddler would love a crawling game that teaches *over, under* and *around* as well. Sing "Charlie Over the WATER" and help your child climb *over* the top of a blanket. (A blue blanket would be great to represent the blue WATER of the ocean if you have one handy.) Play the game again, but ask your child to climb *under* the blanket, or crawl *around* the blanket.

GAMES TO PLAY

Rub a Dub Dub ... Sign Language in a Tub

Materials: plastic cars, animals and balls, shallow plastic bins, sponges, pouring containers

Vocabulary Practice: FISH, WATER, CAR, DOG, CAT

Other Benefits: ability to manipulate objects, sensory experience

Directions: Place plastic versions corresponding to signs the child is learning in a shallow plastic bin filled with one or two inches of water. Cookie cutters make good toys for this game, as do small plastic cars, animals and balls. Be sure to include some objects that float and others that do not. Sponges to squeeze and containers for pouring and filling are great to encourage fine-motor activity.

Sing the lyric, "Charlie catch a FISHIE, can't catch me!" See if your child will find the FISH in the WATER and hand it to you. You can substitute other sign vocabulary for FISHIE, such as race CAR or DOGGIE.

As with all the activities described in this book,
take great care in supervising young children during water play.

Water Bottle Toy

Materials: plastic bottle, water, light corn syrup or vegetable oil, food coloring, sequins or other small objects such as plastic fish, glue gun

Vocabulary Practice: WATER, TOY, FISH

Other Benefits: awareness of cause and effect, focused looking, sensory enjoyment

Directions: Fill a plastic bottle with water and light corn syrup. Add food coloring and glitter as desired. Place small plastic fish in the bottle so that your child can watch them "swim." (Vegetable oil and water may be combined for the same effect.) Firmly attach the water bottle top using a glue gun.

Ask your child if she wants to play with her WATER or FISH TOY. Tell her to watch the FISHIE swim in the WATER. See if she will point to the FISHIE in the bottle when asked.

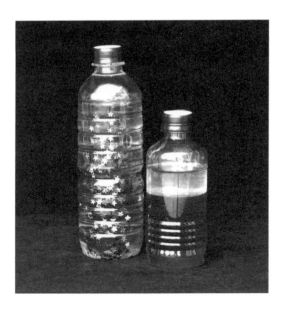

BOOKS TO READ

Arnold, Tedd. *No More Water in the Tub*. New York: Puffin Books, 1998.

Base, Graeme. *The Water Hole*. New York: Puffin Books, 2004.

Johnson, John. *Little Bunny's Bath Time!* Wilton, CT: Tiger Tales, 2004.

Lenski, Lois. *The Little Sailboat*. New York: Random House for Young Readers, 2003.

Milbourne, Anna. *Bunny on the Beach*. Tulsa, OK: Educational Development Corporation Publishing, 2002.

Palmer, Helen and P. D. Eastman. *A Fish out of Water*. New York: Random House Books for Young Readers, 1961.

Peck, Jan. *Way Down Deep in the Deep Blue Sea*. New York: Simon & Schuster Books for Young Readers, 2004.

Penton Overseas. *Rainbow Sea*. Carlsbad, CA: Penton Overseas International, 2001.

Prater, John. *Oh Where, Oh Where?* New York: Scholastic Inc., 1997.

A SIGN OF SUCCESS

Care-Giving Grandmas Get Involved in *Baby Sing & Sign*™

I'll love you dear, I'll love you
Till China and Africa meet,
And the river jumps over the mountain
And the salmon sing in the street.

I'll love you till the ocean
Is folded and hung up to dry
And the seven stars go squawking
Like geese about the sky.

– W.H. AUDEN (1907-1973)

There's something extra special about a grandmother's love – in its constancy and the unconditional way that it's bestowed. Looking back, I know my two grandmothers were some of the greatest blessings of my childhood. My grandmothers made me feel special, made me feel significant, made me feel *heard*. I could talk to my grandmothers about things I would never bring up to my parents. My grandmothers were far less critical.

That is the role of a grandparent. Parents have the responsibility, grandparents have the fun … as well as the perspective that comes from having raised children to adulthood and knowing in retrospect what is truly important. In today's society, more mothers work outside the home and more grandmothers are stepping into the role of caregiver. Sign language can help bridge the communication as well as the generation gap for these grandparents.

Susan keeps her grandson, Quinten, three days a week. She heard about the *Baby Sing & Sign*™ classes and thought taking the class and teaching the signs would help Quinten develop his language skills. "I thought the class was wonderful," Susan said. "I loved the way it was set up and especially enjoyed watching Quinten mixing with the other kids." Quinten and his grandma now listen to the *Baby Sing & Sign*™ CD every day.

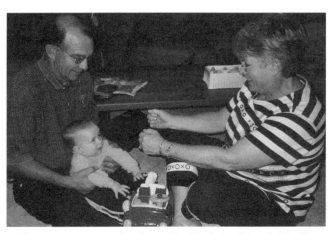

Grandparents get "on board" with *Baby Sing & Sign*™.

Quinten loves the songs and will start clapping as soon as the music begins. Grandma loves how the songs help her remember the signs. "When I turn on the music, I remember the signs," she said.

Karen is her granddaughter's full-time caregiver. She and Allison took the *Baby Sing & Sign*™ class when Allison was eleven months old. "It was fun getting her out," Karen said. "Grandmas can give more attention than parents sometimes can." Allison likes watching her grandma do the signs during the songs. She points to the CD player when she wants to hear the songs. "She definitely enjoys the music," her grandmother noted. "She'll sit and move. She watches me when it's time for the sign – she anticipates what is coming." Almost a year old, Allison can sign PLAY and MORE, the latter especially when she is eating. "Using MORE was a big deal," Susan recalled.

Parents have the responsibility, grandparents have the fun ...

Ann occasionally cares for two grandbabies: Lauren is fifteen months old and her cousin, Sophia, is five weeks younger. The girls took the *Baby Sing & Sign*™ classes with their mothers, but Ann knew she needed to know the signs, too. Ann believes the signing has been very helpful – alleviating a lot of frustration for her grandchildren.

Signing also makes mealtime a cleaner experience at Ann's house. Grandma now waits for Lauren to sign MORE before giving her a second helping of food. When Lauren is finished eating, she signs ALL-DONE and Grandma clears the tray. Before learning to sign, Lauren's method of announcing that the meal was over was to throw any leftover food on the floor. Her grandchildren also now ask to go outside by touching the door and signing PLEASE, a sweet gesture Ann finds difficult to resist.

One day Lauren attended a sporting event with her parents and grandparents in another town. A little bored, the toddler began walking around, eventually joining another family that was seated on a blanket near-by. The father, after asking Lauren's mother for permission, offered Lauren a snack. Ann watched as Lauren ate the snack, then approached the man and signed MORE. She continued making the sign while getting closer and closer to him. "She was talking to him with her sign," Ann said. "And I thought, this little girl knows how to get what she wants within the framework of language she knows."

To babies, Grandmas have always been capable of doing wondrous things. Now, with programs like *Baby Sing & Sign*™, Grandmas and their grandbabies can learn to do wondrous things together.

My World

Words To Learn:
BOOK

Words To Review:
SONG, BALL, PLAY, BOY, GIRL, BED/SLEEP

Tips for introducing *My World*

- Hold the child in your lap and rock side to side as you sing. Demonstrate the signs for your child by holding your hands in front of her body so she can see and touch them.

- Help your child form the signs by gently guiding both her little hands with yours.

- "My World" is a great song for practicing sign language with baby. As you master new signs, you can add verses. Let this be the "theme song" of your signing experience.

- Sign MUSIC on the improvised "loo" verse of the song.

BOOK

Place palms together and then open them as if opening up a book.

Child may either place *palms open or closed*, but not do the opening motion.

My world, my world,
Books for **read**ing in my world
My world, my world,
Books for **read**ing in my world

2. **Songs** for **sing**ing
3. **Balls** for **play**ing
4. Boys and girls
5. **Beds** for **sleeping**
6. Loo Loo... [**music**]

By Anne Meeker Miller

119

More musical fun with *My World*

Items needed: poster board or cardstock paper, pictures representing things or activities from child's life, bulletin board for child's room

- Alter the tempo or quality of the song to keep it musically interesting. For example, try making your singing smoother or more accented as if marching. You could even make the song into a "baby bounce" by adding an up-and-down motion with your knees. Make an even smoother version and exaggerate your swaying from side to side.

- Take a walk around your baby's "world" outdoors. Ask your child to point to things he sees as you travel and make up a new verse for each, such as "grass for growing ..." or "DOGS for petting in my world."

- Make a small poster of pictures that represent important things in your child's life, such as MOMMY, DADDY, DOG or BOOK. Put the poster in a plastic page cover to make it last longer. The pictures on the poster do not need to represent sign language vocabulary, but can be another opportunity for practice. Ask the child to point to a picture on the poster, and then sing a "My World" verse about it.

- You can also make a bulletin board over the changing table consisting of interesting pictures from baby's "world." Change them periodically to maintain his interest.

Mom makes reading an essential
component of Anthony's daily routine.

GAMES TO PLAY

My World Waits

Here is a fun game to play while waiting at a doctor's office, the auto repair shop or some other location not optimally suited for young children to roam. This activity requires no props or preparation. Position the baby in your lap. Once you and baby have learned the "My World" song, hum the melody softly in your baby's ear as if you are telling her a secret. Rock the child gently from side to side as you quietly sing.

When you get to the place in the song where you would sing the words you are learning in sign, place your hands in front of your child and perform the sign. Sing the verses in the sequence you have practiced at home. Depending on the child's age and opportunities to practice, she may anticipate the sign that comes next. That is, she may sign the word that comes next or shape your hands into the sign, indicating that she is able to practice a song internally without support from the lyrics. In its purest form, a child practices the song in her mind without hearing a note. This "singing in your head" activity is great for developing sequencing skills, sign vocabulary and musical memory.

Grandmother Karen sings
quietly to Allison while they
wait at the doctor's office.

Homemade Play Dough

Ingredients:

- 1 cup flour
- 1 cup warm water
- 2 teaspoons cream of tartar
- 1 teaspoon oil
- 1/4 cup salt
- food coloring, flavoring, spices or Kool-Aid™ drink mix if desired

Vocabulary Practice: PLAY, ALL-DONE, DOG, CAT, BALL, FISH

Other Benefits: tactile stimulation, creativity

Directions: Mix all ingredients together, adding food coloring last. Stir over medium heat until smooth and forming a ball in the pan. As soon as it is cool enough to handle, remove dough from pan and knead. Place in plastic bag or airtight container when cooled. The dough will last for a long time.

Variations:

- Put in two packages of Kool-Aid™ to add smell as well as color.
- Include food coloring and spices to provide more sensory interest for your child such as cinnamon, pumpkin pie spice, or extracts such as peppermint, lemon, orange or strawberry.

Ask your child if she would like to PLAY with PLAY dough. Help her roll the dough and use cookie cutters in the shape of DOG, CAT, BALL or FISH. Watch for her to tell you she is ALL-DONE with her dough play.

The coolness and texture of
the play dough provides
"finger fun" for Isaac.

BOOKS TO READ

Most parents of young children are familiar with the wonderful picture book *Goodnight Moon*. Margaret Wise Brown wrote another book called *My World* (HarperFestival Publishers, 1949) that shares the same style of prose and illustration. Both you and your child will enjoy reading *My World*. Its text embeds much of the sign vocabulary selected for the *Baby Sing & Sign™* program, providing an interesting way to practice sign language.

MORE BOOKS TO READ

Bertram, Debbie and Susan Bloom. *The Best Place to Read*. New York: Random House, 2003.

Browne, Anthony. *I Like Books*. Cambridge, MA: Candlewick Press, 1988.

DK Kids. *Baby's World: Ready, Set, Go!* New York: DK Publishing Inc., 2004.

Fox, Mem. *Whoever You Are*. New York: Voyager Books, 2001.

Hoffelt, Jane E. *We Share One World*. Bellevue, WA: Illumination Arts Publishing Co., Inc., 2004.

Miller, J. Philip and Sheppard M. Greene. *We All Sing with the Same Voice*. New York: HarperCollins Publishers, 1982.

A SIGN OF SUCCESS

Sign as a Second Language:
Children Building Bridges of Understanding
Between Deaf and Hearing Cultures

One-year-old Ava and her family were enjoying a dinner at their favorite restaurant. Ava's parents were "chatting" with her using the baby signs she had enthusiastically mastered. Also enjoying a meal out that evening was a group of older deaf adults. They approached the family to ask whether Ava was deaf and began to have a conversation using sign language, lip reading and pantomime.

Ava's mother was able to sign BABY, and the deaf adults taught her the sign for SIGN. Ava and her family shared their entire repertoire of sign vocabulary, including all the animals they had learned, to the amusement and amazement of the deaf adults, who in turn taught the family some new signs. Ava's parents sensed that the deaf adults were thrilled and grateful that sign language was an essential part of the daily lives of a hearing family. One member of the group assured Ava's mother that signing would "increase the baby's intelligence." It was a wonderful experience for all.

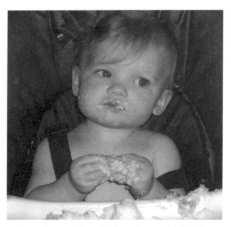

Ava shared her baby sign – MORE – with her new deaf friends.

The benefits of using signs based on American Sign Language (ASL) with babies are numerous. This form of signed communication uses hand shapes that are simple to use and more compatible with baby's developing fine-motor skills. The prevalence of ASL in the United States, and its popularity as a communication system with hearing as well as deaf children, makes the gestures easily recognizable as children move from home to daycare, or change from one daycare setting to another.

Darcy is a deaf educator who works primarily with deaf toddlers. She taught her three hearing daughters baby sign and teaches classes and workshops on sign language to hearing children. She has used the *Baby Sing & Sign™* program extensively with her students who have received cochlear implants, and reports that it has been helpful in teaching them how to listen. For example, "This Is the Mommy Wiggle" helps students recognize the difference in the vocal qualities of a man, woman and child. "The Little Cat Goes Creeping" helps them hear changing tempi or speed fluctuations in the music. In addition, she thinks the program's emphasis on focused listening has been invaluable to her students and finds that hearing children experience the same benefits. Just as for hearing children, a combination of speech and sign is used to realize the goal of spoken communication.

Robin is an interpreter and preschool teacher at a state school for deaf students. She is also the mother of a deaf child. She believes that ASL sets the tone for language development, and allows hearing and deaf children to acquire communication skills in a natural way. The hand shapes are "unmarked," which means they require no knowledge of the signed alphabet. They give children communication facility that is precise, immediate and easily recognized by family members and caregivers, as well as those in the deaf community.

Robin and Darcy agree that baby signing has been greeted enthusiastically by the deaf community. The hope is that teaching young hearing children to sign will help to break down stereotypes and barriers. Russian psychologist Lev Vygotsky called attention to the dependence of learning on interaction and cooperation between children. The reality is that, as Cohen (1995) noted, social communication between hearing and deaf children in school settings can be a negative experience. The deaf child feels like an outsider and the hearing child is uncertain or fearful of what is expected of him. Therefore, teaching hearing children to sign to their deaf peers will help all children feel included and their contributions valued.

The prevalence of ASL in the United States, and its popularity as a communication system with hearing as well as deaf children, makes the gestures easily recognizable.

Many secondary and some elementary schools are starting to include ASL instruction in their curriculum. With the move toward inclusion of all children in the general education classroom, regardless of their disability, there is an increased likelihood that hearing and deaf children will have the opportunity to interact and learn together. Giving hearing children the tools to communicate with their deaf peers will provide a bridge of understanding that will lead to shared experience and mutual respect.

And that spells friendship in any language.

Cohen, Oscar. "The Adverse Implications of Full Inclusion for Deaf Students." In *Proceedings of the International Congress on Education of the Deaf* (18th, Tel Aviv, July 16-20, 1995).

Vygotsky, Lev. *Mind in Society*. Cambridge, MA: Harvard University Press, 1978.

13
Skye Boat Song

Words To Learn:
STARS, BLANKET, MOON, I LOVE YOU

Words To Review:
MUSIC, WATER

Tips for introducing *Skye Boat Song*

- The song can be a "listening" lullaby for you and your baby. The violin playing is beautiful and very soothing. Dim the lights and snuggle into a rocking chair. Rock rhythmically and gently in time with the tune.

- Gently add the signs for STARS, BLANKET and MOON as you sing the lyrics or hum the tune.

- When the violin plays its special solo section, you can sign MUSIC for baby to see. Always conclude the song with an I LOVE YOU hug.

- Hum or sing quietly in your child's ear.

STARS

Move both lifted pointers up and down "in the sky."

Child may lift one hand or both and wiggle fingers over head.

Speed, bonnie boat, like a bird on the wing.
"Onward," the sailors cry.
Carry the babe that's born to be king over the sea to Skye.
Bright the **stars** shine.
Lightly we sail.
Quiet the waves roll by.
Blanket for baby, hug and a kiss.
Moon sings a lullaby.

Traditional
Adapted by Anne Meeker Miller

127

More Musical Fun with *Skye Boat Song*

- This lovely old ballad tells the story of Bonnie Prince Charlie, who escaped from the Scottish mainland to the Island of Skye after he was defeated in battle.

- Set aside any misguided belief you hold that you are not a good enough singer to sing to your children. They believe you are the best singer in the world. They associate you with smiles, kisses, good smells and beautiful music. There is no voice they prefer to yours.

- Provide a prelude to this bedtime lullaby by singing the song during bathtime. Add a boat to your bath toys and let your child be the boat's captain! This practice provides a lovely and natural transition from bath to bedtime rituals.

BLANKET

Two hands pretend
to pull a blanket up
to beneath chin.

Moon Walk with Baby

My firstborn son received most of the toys available commercially during his first two years of life. Such is the fate of a first grandchild! Among all these riches, one of his favorite "toys" was the actual, honest-to-goodness MOON (the one you see in the sky on a cloudless night).

My husband made a game of searching our backyard with Andy, looking for the moon. He would tell our son the Russians had stolen it when the MOON was nowhere to be found. (My apologies to the Russians, who are wonderful people. My husband watches too many James Bond movies.)

There is something magical about the MOON. Hum or sing "Skye Boat Song" to your child out under the moonlight on a mild evening.

Form "C" with pointer and thumb, and lift this "crescent moon" over head.

MOON

Child may simply lift hand over head.

Smooth Sailing

The structure and predictability of music is comforting to your child, as is the sight and scent of you. From the perspective of babies, there is very little in their world that they can control. The events of their lives seem to be a constant bombardment of random activity. That is why your nighttime routine is such a cherished part of their day. They can expect that after a bath and a nighttime bottle or snack come books and holding.

WATER was the first sign "Bonnie Prince" Andrew's parents observed him use in signed communication with them.

Your child enjoys the sensation of your singing. With his back to your chest, he can feel you breathe and experience the resonance of your singing against his skin. This will remind him of a time not long ago when you rocked him as he floated in the womb, and when the distant sound of your voice was the only music he knew. The rhythm of your singing was the beat of your heart.

Rock on.

Both *closed fists* cross chest, as if hugging self.

I LOVE YOU

Child may pat upper chest with palms.

BOOKS TO READ

Boynton, Sandra. *Snuggle Puppy!* New York: Workman Publishing Co., Inc., 2003.

Brown, Margaret Wise. *Sailor Boy Jig.* New York: Simon and Schuster, 2002.

Cusimano, Mary Ann K. and Satomi Ichikawa. *You Are My I Love You.* New York: Philomel Books, 2001.

Davis, Billy. *Shake the Maracas!* New York: Scholastic Inc., 2000.

Dillard, Sarah. *Ten Wishing Stars: A Countdown to Bedtime Book.* Los Angeles: Piggy Toes Press, 2003.

Morse, Simon. *Get Ready to Sail* (Bathtub Book). Norwalk, CT: Innovative Kids, 2002.

Joel, Billy. *Goodnight My Angel.* New York: Scholastic Press, 2004.

Mack, Lizzie. *Give a Little Love.* New York: Little Simon, 2004.

Otoshi, Kathryn. *What Emily Saw.* San Rafael, CA: KO Kids Books, 2003.

Spinelli, Eileen. *Rise the Moon.* New York: Dial Books for Young Readers, 2003.

Van Genechten, Guido. *Because I Love You So Much.* Wilton, CT: Tiger Tales, 2004.

A SIGN OF SUCCESS
The Art of Expecting Nothing

Our children are like butterflies –
quite beautiful in their own ways, in their own time.
They should not be pushed to preen,
or to fly, before they are ready.

– ALVIN ROSENFELD AND NICOLE WISE

Often the unique soul of a child gets lost amid all the pushing and directing and orchestration of its upbringing. Children want nothing more than to please their parents and will go to great lengths to try not to let them down, even if it is holding them back from what they'd rather be doing.

There's a saying I've always loved – something about how parents don't own their children, God just loans them for eighteen years. Part of the delight in being in the company of kids is the opportunity to see them as the unique individuals they are: what gifts they were born with, what lessons they are here to teach us and what lessons we can help them learn.

For that reason, I believe the best role parents can play is that of guide. By introducing them to the world, answering their questions, accepting them with an open heart and exposing them to a wide range of experiences, parents allow

There is great value in quiet moments.

children freedom to find their own opportunities to blossom and grow.

As William Crain, Ph.D., points out in his book *Reclaiming Childhood*, with each passing year our society is placing greater importance on preparing children for their life as adults instead of just embracing and enjoying them during this youthful and creative time in their lives. Writes Crain, "in today's world children's present interests and feelings count for little in comparison to the all-important goal of preparing them for the adult workplace" (p. 2). Crain goes on, "We are so preoccupied with their future that we cannot see and value them for who they are, children" (p. 6).

Cindy Giddings has a master's degree in special education, has facilitated a Parents as Teachers Program and is co-creator of the *Baby Sing & Sign*™ program. As the mother of a young son, she is increasingly troubled by what she sees as a generation of children who are grossly over-scheduled. "I'm beginning to see parenting skill measured by how many activities parents schedule for their kids," she commented. "One does not accurately reflect the other."

She believes children are so over-scheduled and spend so much time being shuffled from place to place that they are often lost and don't know what to do during the rare quiet moment. Giddings stressed that just spending time with your baby, holding her and looking in her eyes, making her feel infinitely loved and cared for will help her immeasurably as she grows older. "There's great value in quiet moments," she noted.

In fact, we may be robbing our children of inner peace and contentment if we don't allow them quiet moments for individual creative pursuits and time spent outdoors studying nature. According to Crain, "a small but growing body of research suggests that childhood is indeed a time of special sensitivity to nature. It seems that up to the age of twelve, children have a great urge to explore and find comfort in natural settings" (p. 5). By keeping kids electronically stimulated with computers, videos and television, and not letting them outdoors to ramble through woods or throw rocks in a pond, Crain believes we are "in effect, stunting their growth."

"Find your child's passion and pursue it ... offer enhancing opportunities when appropriate and easy to do."

Authors Alvin Rosenfeld and Nicole Wise write in their book *Hyper-Parenting: Are You Hurting Your Child by Trying Too Hard?* that "it is tough to try to be relaxed, especially when we so desperately fear being negligent. What we parents really need as much as, or perhaps even more than, all that important advice about how to raise our children is a reminder that no one ever gets it all just right – and that most children turn out well anyway" (p. 5).

I believe one of the biggest responsibilities parents have is recognizing each child's God-given talents and doing all they can to nurture them. Giddings agrees. "Find your child's passion and pursue it ... offer enhancing opportunities when appropriate and easy to do. It doesn't have to be pre-scheduled," she adds.

How does this relate to *Baby Sing & Sign*™, you ask? Simply put, you may think the idea of teaching babies to sign is the greatest thing ever. However, be open to the possibility that your infant has other ideas. It may not be her cup of tea. Or it may suit her just fine, but not at eight months, twelve months or even sixteen.

Sign language cannot be force-fed. The beauty of the *Baby Sing & Sign*™ program is that it can be incorporated into naturally occurring life situations, such as in the car and during mealtimes. Although taking a *Baby Sing & Sign*™ class is great fun, the program can also be home-based and home-taught.

The information in this book is intended to give you, as teacher and guide, the tools and activities you need to help your baby learn sign language. The rules are not set in stone. The timeline isn't concrete. What worked for your best friend's son may not have any impact on your daughter. That's okay. You have not failed as a parent or teacher, and most certainly your child hasn't failed you.

"Expect nothing and you will never be disappointed." How easy that is to say and how difficult it is to put into daily practice. But, for the sake of your children, it's important to try. Because childhood is not merely preparation for the future, but a time that is precious and valuable in its own right.

Crain, William. *Reclaiming Childhood.* New York: Henry Holt and Co. LLC, 2003.

Rosenfeld, Alvin and Nicole Wise. *Hyper-Parenting: Are You Hurting Your Child by Trying Too Hard?* New York: St. Martin's Press, 2000.

14
Lady, Lady Lullaby

Words To Review:
SLEEP/BED, I LOVE YOU

Tips for introducing *Lady, Lady Lullaby*

- Hold your child as you stand and sway.

- A cappella singing refers to singing without instrumental accompaniment. "Lady, Lady" is an example of a cappella performance. Children learn to sing accurately when presented with unaccompanied singing as instruments appear to distract them from hearing and processing the melody of a song. Sing the lullaby softly. Hearing your unaccompanied singing voice is all your baby needs to start fine-tuning her own singing skills.

- If your back is sturdy, bend your knees or dip your child gently on "sweep them low" and lift her up a bit on "sweep them high." From a seated position, you can also pantomime the sweeping broom with arms reaching high and low.

- Conclude the song with a warm embrace of your child and perhaps a gentle spin. Tell your child I LOVE YOU. However, the sweetness of this experience for your child will communicate your feelings more expressively than your spoken words.

LADY, LADY LULLABY

Lady, lady, buy a broom for my baby.
Lady, lady, buy a broom for my baby.
Sweep them low, sweep them high,
Sweep the cobwebs out of the sky.
Lady, lady, buy a broom for my baby.

More musical fun with *Lady, Lady Lullaby*

- The benefits of singing lullabies to your child have more to do with strengthening the bond between the two of you and providing comfort than with developing musical or language skills.

- Your nighttime ritual should include a repertoire of lullabies that will be part of your family's tradition.

- Remember that you are your child's first and best music teacher. The lullabies you sing with your children will be the same ones they will sing to their own babies.

- Be consistent with your nighttime rituals. Do not skip any steps, and most certainly do not forget to sing!

- Lullabies are the ultimate expressive experience. Parents are able to communicate deep affection for their child in a way that only music makes possible.

Heather loves the predictability and comfort
her bedtime routine provides.

BOOKS TO READ

Boynton, Sandra. *Snoozers*. New York: Little Simon, 1997.

Butler, John. *While You Were Sleeping*. Atlanta, GA: Peachtree Publishers, Ltd., 2001.

Child, Lauren. *I Am Not Sleepy and I Will Not Go to Bed*. Cambridge, MA: Candlewick Press, 2001.

Couri, Kathy. *Goodnight Bear*. Santa Monica, CA: Piggy Toes Press, 1999.

Degen, Bruce. *Jamberry Board Book*. New York: HarperFestival Publishers, 1994.

Fleming, Denise. *Time to Sleep*. New York: Henry Holt and Company, 2001.

Vere, Ed. *Everyone's Sleepy*. New York: Orchard Books, 2001.

Wood, Audrey. *The Napping House: Lap-Sized Board Book*. New York: Red Wagon Books, 2005.

A SIGN OF SUCCESS
Children, Music and Miracles

It was the poet and philosopher J. K. Rowling who said, "Ah, music. A magic beyond all we do here!"*

There is something mystical and profoundly unpredictable in the ways children begin to express their musical selves. I have never met a baby who didn't adore music. A child's developing awareness of music in all its forms – from Bach to Britney – can provide some remarkable moments for those of us fortunate enough to witness them.

Fifteen-month-old Bennett was a confident walker and spent the majority of his time on the move. As a member of a *Baby Sing & Sign*™ class, he was keenly interested in the music and play portion of the program, but seemed only marginally interested in the sign language instruction. His mother, Rebecca, began to teach Bennett some basic sign vocabulary, starting with MORE, MUSIC and FISH. She was patient and consistent with her signing, but not certain that Bennett was even watching as she signed and spoke.

A child's developing awareness of music in all its forms – from Bach to Britney – can provide some remarkable moments for those of us fortunate enough to witness them.

Shortly after starting the class, Rebecca was listening to the funeral ceremony for former President Ronald Reagan on television. Elsewhere in the room, her son was busy playing with his toys as usual, and appeared to pay no attention to the television program. But when a choir began to perform during the ceremony, Bennett set down his toys and walked to his mother. He looked at the television set and signed MUSIC. This was an amazing moment for her.

Some scientists suggest that babies are biologically "pre-wired" to respond to certain classes of sound, and that was perhaps the reason why Bennett recognized that both the choral performance and his baby sign songs were "music."

For me, the image of a toddler signing MUSIC for the first time in response to a musical event that occurred in a "picture box," camouflaged in a musical form he had never experienced, is nothing short of miraculous. It reminds me of the difference between thinking and learning. I am humbled with the knowledge that babies are often their own best teachers.

… And so grateful to be a part of Bennett's life.

---

*J. K. Rowling. *Harry Potter and the Sorcerer's Stone*. New York: Scholastic, 1998.

BOOKS
Baby Sign and Language Development

Acredolo, Linda and Susan Goodwyn. *Baby Minds*. New York: Bantam Books, 2000.

——. *Baby Signs*. Chicago: Contemporary Books, 1996.

Bahan, Ben and Joe Dannis. *Signs for Me: Basic Sign Vocabulary for Children, Parents & Teachers*. San Diego, CA: Dawn Sign Press, 1990.

Baker, Pamela and Patricia B. Bellen Gillen. *My First Book of Sign*. Washington, DC: Gallaudet University Press, 2002.

Daniels, Marilyn. *Dancing with Words: Signing for Hearing Children's Literacy*. Westport, CT: Bergin & Garvey, 2001.

Garcia, Joseph. *Sign with Your Baby: How to Communicate with Infants Before They Can Speak*. Seattle, WA: Northlight Communications and Bellingham, Washington: Stratton-Kehl Publications, Inc., 1999.

Gardner, Howard. *Frames of Mind*. New York: Basic Books, 1993.

——. *Intelligence Reframed: Multiple Intelligences for the 21st Century*. New York: Basic Books, 2000.

Golinkoff, Roberta M. and Kathy Hirsh-Pasek. *How Babies Talk: The Magic and Mystery of Language in the First Three Years of Life*. New York: Penguin Group, 1999.

Gopnik, Alison, Andrew N. Meltoff and Patricia Kuhl. *The Scientist in the Crib: What Early Learning Tells Us About the Mind*. New York: HarperCollins Publishers, 1999.

Hafer, Jan, Robert Wilson and Paul Setzer. *Come Sign With Us: Sign Language Activities for Children*. Washington, DC: Gallaudet University Press, 2002.

Slier, Debby. *Animal Signs*. Washington, DC: Gallaudet University Press, 2002.

Stewart, David. *American Sign Language the Easy Way*. Hauppauge, NY: Barron's Educational Series, 1998.

Books
Music for Young Children

Appleby, Amy and Peter Pickow, ed. *The Library of Children's Song Classics*. New York: Amsco Publications, 1993.

Bradford, Louise L., ed. *Sing It Yourself: 220 Pentatonic American Folk Songs*. Sherman Oaks, CA: Alfred Publishing Company, 1978.

Brown, Marc. *Hand Rhymes*. New York: Penguin Books, 1985.

Campbell, Don. *The Mozart Effect for Children: Awakening Your Child's Mind, Health, and Creativity with Music*. New York: HarperCollins Publishers, 2000.

Cole, William, ed. *Folk Songs of England, Ireland, Scotland & Wales*. Garden City, NY: Doubleday & Company, Inc., 1961.

Feierabend, John M., ed. *Music for Very Little People*. New York: Boosey & Hawkes, 1986.

——. *The Book of Lullabies*. Chicago: GIA Steps, Inc., 2000.

——. *The Book of Simple Songs & Circles*. Chicago: GIA Steps, Inc., 2000.

——. *The Book of Tapping & Clapping*. Chicago: GIA Steps, Inc., 2000.

——. *The Book of Wiggles & Tickles*. Chicago: GIA Steps, Inc., 2000.

Fox, Dan, ed. *Go In and Out the Window: An Illustrated Songbook for Young People*. New York: The Metropolitan Museum of Art and Henry Holt & Company, 1987.

Glazer, Tom. *Music for Ones and Twos: Songs and Games for the Very Young Child*. New York: Doubleday Books, 1983.

A child is never too young to develop a love for books and reading.

Langstaff, Nancy and John Langstaff, eds. *Jim Along, Josie: A Collection of Folk Songs and Singing Games for Young Children.* New York: Harcourt Brace Jovanovich Inc., 1970.

Lomax, John and Alan Lomax, eds. *Best Loved American Folk Songs.* New York: Grosset & Dunlap Publishers, 1947.

——. *Our Singing Country: Folk Songs and Ballads.* New York: Dover Publications, 1941.

Orff-Schulwerk American Edition Volume 1. *Music for Children: Preschool.* Miami, FL: Schott Music Corporation, 1982.

Ortiz, John. *Nurturing Your Child with Music: How Sound Awareness Creates Happy, Smart, and Confident Children.* Hillsboro, OR: Beyond Words Publishing, 1999.

Piazza, Carolyn L. *Multiple Forms of Literacy: Teaching Literacy and the Arts.* Upper Saddle River, NJ: Prentice-Hall, Inc., 1999.

Sandburg, Carl, ed. *The American Songbag.* New York: Harcourt, Brace & World, Inc., 1927.

Seeger, Ruth Crawford, ed. *American Folk Songs for Children.* New York: Doubleday & Company, 1948.

——. *Animal Folk Songs for Children.* Hamden, CT: Linnet Books, 1950.

Simon, William L., ed. *The Reader's Digest Children's Songbook.* Pleasantville, NY: The Reader's Digest Association, Inc., 1985.

Winn, Marie, ed. *The Fireside Book of Children's Songs.* New York: Simon & Schuster, 1966.

WEBSITES

ASL Browser
http://commtechlab.msu.edu/sites/aslweb/browser.htm
This site provides hundreds of one-word video clips and instruction of ASL signs.

Baby Fingers
http://www.mybabyfingers.com/
A music and sign language program based in New York City.

Baby Signs
http://www.babysigns.com/
The official site for Acredolo and Goodwyn's Baby Signs program.

Berkeley Parents Network
http://parents.berkeley.edu/advice/babies/signing.html
Forum for parents to offer advice and comments about their experiences with baby sign.

Handspeak
http://www.handspeak.com/
Information about baby sign is included at this site for learning visual languages.

John Feierabend's Early Childhood Music Program
www.giamusic.com/
Information about the philosophy, research and teaching materials of one of the country's preeminent authorities on music for young children.

Kinder Signs
http://www.kindersigns.com/
An Orlando, Florida-based program founded by speech pathologist Diane Ryan devoted to teaching parents how to communicate with their babies before they can speak.

Love Language™
http://www.lovelanguageforbabies.com/
The official website for the Kansas City-based Love Language™ program. Information about research, classes and instructional products.

Peggy Seeger
www.pegseeger.com/
Stories, humor and information by Ms. Seeger about her experiences as a songwriter, singer, and member of the famous folk-singing Seeger family.

Sign 2 Me
http://www.sign2me.com/
Information about Joseph Garcia's "Sign with your Baby" program.

What Research Says About
Singing and Signing with Your Baby

For those interested in findings from the scientific community regarding including sign language instruction and music in the lives of young children, excerpts from some notable research studies are provided below.

"Symbolic gestures are very similar, if not virtually equivalent, to early vocal words. They are used, just as early words are, to label objects as diverse as tractors and trees, rabbits and rain. And they are frequently combined with other symbols – including words – to communicate more complex ideas. In addition to these similarities in function we have also learned that both symbolic gestures and symbolic words arrive on the scene at the end of the first year, on average, with gestures having a slight edge for many children and a greater edge for a few."

Goodwyn, Susan and Linda Acredolo. "Encouraging symbolic gestures: Effects on the relationship between gesture and speech." In J. Iverson and S. Goldin-Meadows, eds. *The Nature and Functions of Gesture in Children's Communication* (San Francisco: Jossey-Bass, 1998), 61-73.

"Students who receive sign instruction test significantly higher on the Peabody Picture Vocabulary Test than students in classes not receiving sign instruction. Their superior scores indicate that simultaneously presenting words visually, kinesthetically, and orally enhances a child's language development."

Daniels, Marilyn. *Dancing with Words* (Westport, CT: Bergin & Garvey, 2001), 33.

"The infant vocal tract is not simply a miniature version of an adult's. Rather, it resembles the vocal tract of nonhuman primates. This prevents babies from using the mouth as an instrument in the ways necessary for speech. Not until the end of the first year of life, when the oral cavity has lengthened and expanded, are babies able to produce language sounds."

Golinkoff, Roberta M. and Kathy Hirsch-Pasek. *How Babies Talk: The Magic and Mystery of Language in the First Three Years of Life* (New York: Plume, 1997), 40.

"The research literature on music enrichment for infants and toddlers has been prolific. We know that music participation teaches music skills, perception, and cognition. Simultaneously it also promotes child development areas such as listening skills, language development, motor coordination, cooperative social skills and reciprocity, demonstrating the power of music to be a highly beneficial reinforcer for children from the moment of their birth."

Standley, Jayne. "The power of contingent music for infant learning." *Bulletin of the Council for Research in Music Education*, 147 (Spring, 2001), 65-85.

GLOSSARY

American Sign Language (ASL) – widely accepted communication system using gestures

Approximation – close resemblance to an object or event (e.g., sign formation, a desired melody)

Autism – brain disorder characterized by impairment of social relationships, inappropriate or exaggerated responses to stimuli and/or abnormal language development

Caregiver – person other than the parent who cares for children (e.g., sitter, other family member)

Cause and effect – understanding that one action results in a reaction or consequence (e.g., if a child pushes a ball, it will roll)

Cochlear implant – hearing aid implanted in the inner ear that restores hearing to some people with hearing loss

Developmentally appropriate – skills or knowledge that fall within the range of what can typically be expected of someone at a certain age

Expressive language – use of words and/or gestures to communicate with others

Marked hand shape – sign language gestures that incorporate a letter of the signed alphabet

Neocortex – part of the brain that controls thinking (including reasoning, language and problem solving). It can be physiologically altered through sensory experiences and learning.

Baby Sing & Sign™ enhances the bond between parent or caregiver and child.

Neural fibers – structures that enable nerve cells (neurons) to transmit signals to and receive signals from other nerve cells. Neural connections are the basis for learning, and experience can change their strength and efficiency

Object permanence – a child's ability to understand that objects still exist even when they are no longer in sight. Children younger than eight months typically do not have this ability.

Receptive language – ability to understand and organize language

Sequencing skills – ability to order objects using a rule or pattern (e.g., smallest to largest)

Synapse – gap between nerve cells (neurons). Neurons communicate with other neurons by electrochemical activity in which various chemicals (neurotransmitters) are fired or sent across synapses. Synaptic activity is a part of learning, indeed of life.

Tactile stimulation – feedback received from touch

Unmarked hand shape – sign language gestures that do not incorporate a letter of the signed alphabet

ABOUT THE AUTHOR

Anne Meeker Miller, Ph.D., is the founder of the Love Language™ Program. She teaches *Baby Sing & Sign*™ series and seminars at a major medical center in the Kansas City area. Through her writing and workshops, she shares information about the benefits of music, sign language and play for babies, and gives easy and practical strategies for embedding all three into the daily lives of families.

Anne is a music therapist for the early childhood special education program of the Blue Valley School District in Overland Park, Kansas. Her preschool students were the inspiration for her work with sign language and music. Anne observed the way song and sign positively impacted the language skills of her students and wanted to have an influence even earlier in the lives of children when language is first acquired.

Anne has taught music to students from preschool through college levels. She received the Excellence in Teaching Award given by the Learning Exchange, Kansas City Chamber of Commerce and *The Kansas City Star* and is the recipient of the 2004 Kansas Educator of the Year in Arts and Disabilities Award given by Accessible Arts, Inc., and the Kansas State Board of Education. She was a commission member of the Housewright Symposium on the Future of Music Education sponsored by the Music Educators National Conference.

A graduate of the University of Kansas, Anne earned a Ph.D. in music education and music therapy. She holds national board certification in music therapy from the American Music Therapy Association. Anne lives in Olathe, Kansas, where she enjoys spending time with her husband, three sons and Wheaten terrier, Cooper.

CONTRIBUTORS

Carrie Kent, Co-Author of "A Sign of Success" Stories

Carrie Kent holds a bachelor of science degree in journalism from the University of Kansas, where she first met the author. Anne Meeker Miller and Carrie Kent spent a lot of time in college seated at a piano, with Anne playing the piano and singing and Carrie watching raptly, wishing she could play the piano and sing.

Though tone-deaf, Carrie has extensive experience as a writer, editor and proofreader for a variety of print publications, including magazines, newspapers and newsletters. She writes about real estate for *The Kansas City Star*. Her earlier professional experience included stints as an associate editor for *The Mother Earth News* magazine and a research and administrative assistant for two prominent columnists in the Washington, DC, bureau of *The Wall Street Journal*. She has also been employed as a live-in nanny (among the happiest years of her life) and continues to work as a babysitter with Nannies of Kansas City, Ltd. Carrie's childcare experience and writing skills have come together for this project of describing the wonderful world of babies who learned to sign through music and play.

When she isn't working, writing or playing with children, Carrie enjoys baking, cooking and decorating her home. Her four pets keep her busy, as does corresponding with close friends who live in other states.

Jeff Petrie, Illustrator

Jeff Petrie has been interested in drawing ever since he was a child. He studied graphic design at Johnson County Community College in Overland Park, Kansas. He has provided graphic design work for Glynn Devins Advertising and Marketing, as well as the Headache and Pain Center in Overland Park, Kansas. A piece of his artwork was featured at the Muscular Dystrophy Association (MDA) national headquarters, and his Christmas card illustration was chosen for the Muscular Dystrophy Association's Holiday Wishes Collection in 2000 and 2003. Jeff received the MDA Personal Achievement Award for the Kansas City area and the state of Kansas.

Jeff enjoys listening to and collecting music, going to concerts, surfing the Internet and hanging out with friends. He lives in Overland Park, Kansas, with his family and two dogs, Einstein and Hailey. His whimsical illustrations are a wonderful addition to this book.

Amy Martin, Photographer

After a previous life as a computer software designer and several wonderful years at home raising her three beautiful daughters, Amy Martin decided to follow her passion and began a new career as a portrait photographer. With the encouragement and support of her family and friends, she started a small studio in the Kansas City area, where she spends her time capturing the magic and innocence of small children.

Amy lives in Olathe, Kansas, with her husband, daughters, and a small menagerie of four-legged friends. Her photographs are a wonderful enhancement for this program and get to the heart of the playfulness and fun we aspire to share with our readers.

ACKNOWLEDGMENTS

The following "cast" of performers, editors, photograph models and parenting experts deserve a standing ovation for their help with this project:

Denise Ahnen
Dr. Lynn Brinckmeyer
Darcie Blake
Julie Bolton
Julie Broski
Malinda Bryan-Smith
Claudia Burford
Terry Busch
Dr. David Circle
Ruth Davidson
Cyndi Fahrlander
Stephanie Faoro
Judy Farinelli
Jim Giddings
Charles Golladay
Tony Harper
Kirsten Herman
Gina Hicklin
Jan Holthus
Mark Kohlhase
Dr. Chris Lessly
Nancy Milner
Laura Murphy
Mary Licktieg
Amy Lind
Robin Olson
Janet Railton
Twila Samborski
Danielle Tyler
Theresa Watson
Parents and children of the Blue Valley
    School District
Baby Sing & Sign™ class participants
The Meeker and Miller families all

Pictured in text:

Megan and William Baum
Jack Bryan
Brad, Isaac and Kendall Burr
Ava Clayton
Anthony and Edda Concessi
Josie and Max Faoro
Gilli Gerson
Brady Hale
Megan and Emery Hankins
Ella Hans
Kreg and Lana Herman
Jaylie Hicklin
Jillian Lewis
Allison and Karen McNellis
Turi and Al Melichar
Heather Metcalf
Greg, Kevin, Andy and Cooper Miller
Ermil Miller
Anna Munley
Peyton Ott
Jaclynn Pickens and Edie Howard
Justa, Keith, Lea and Richard
    Plantenberg
Deirdre Poague
Lucy and Tracy Powell
Mac Rodrick
Naomi Routien
Gianni and Isabella Scavuzzo
Nathan and Nicholas Siscoe
Andrew Stark
Hannah and Melinda Young

Special Thanks To:

Cindy Giddings for lovingly building *Baby Sing & Sign*™ with me

"Team *BS&S*" for expert counsel, hand-holding, lots of hard work, and dreaming out loud with me: Kendall Burr, Barb Harper, Amy Scavuzzo and Melinda Young

Pola Zenitsky Firestone for teaching the teacher to be an author, and Kirsten McBride for wielding her red pen with such precision and zest

Carrie Kent for loving this project as much as its "mother" does

Darcy Beaver, Loni Herrera, Gayle Kebodeux and Wendy Webb for their encouragement, wisdom and input

Kelly Werts, my musical muse and most talented friend

Jeff Petrie, Amy Martin and Kim Tappan for all the visual treats this book contains

Rudolf E. Radocy, Ph.D., for his assistance with the glossary, and his wise reminder that "complex things can only be simplified so far"

My fairy godmother and magical girlfriend, Marjorie Lamb Gamble

Megan Hankins and Lana Herman, my sign language "super models"

Chelcy Bowles, Karl Bruhn, Kim Burns, Jim Byo, Richard Chronister, Rob Cuttietta, Randy DeWitt, June Hinckley, Judith Jellison, Marvelene Moore and other esteemed commission members of the Housewright Symposium for their mentorship and influence in shaping my own "Vision 2020"

Alice-Ann Darrow, my official "cheerleader" and advisor for life

My "real" father, Donald

My lovely "other mother," Loretta Miller and her beau, Ermil R. Miller

My sister, Donna, who is the woman I want to be when I grow up

My prince-of-a-husband, Dan, and our fine "babies," Greg, Kevin and Andy

Love Language™
Presents

Clap Your Hands
Play-Filled Songs
for Little Children

The companion music CD to

BABY SING & SIGN™
*A Play-Filled Language Development Program
for Hearing Infants and Toddlers*

by Anne Meeker Miller, Ph.D.

This music CD includes a wonderful variety of toe-tapping tunes sure to engage the minds, motors and hearts of singers young and old. The melodies are childlike and catchy, with just the right number of instruments and ideas for baby's developing musical awareness. Yet, they are interesting and fun for adults as well.

- The CD provides a rich musical repertoire that complements the emerging musical abilities of young children.

- By learning these lovely songs together, you can build a tradition of music making in your family or daycare, and strengthen the bond between you and the children you love and care for.

More information about *Baby Sing and Sign*™ products may be found on the next page of this book or at our website:

www.babysingandsign.com

Order Form
Baby Sing & Sign™ Products

Please send me:

BABY SING & SIGN™ BOOK AND MUSIC CD: *A Play-Filled Language Development Program for Hearing Infants and Toddlers*

Book and companion music CD for parents, grandparents and caregivers

Quantity: _____ at $34.95 each + shipping at $3.00 each = _____

NOTE: *You receive a 10% discount on the purchase price when you order 2 or more sets.*

CLAP YOUR HANDS: *Play-Filled Songs for Little Children* Music CD

Quantity: _____ at $14.95 each + shipping at $3.00 each = _____

GRAND TOTAL: _____

Please print.

Name: _____

Address: _____

City: _____ State: _____ Zip: _____

Telephone: _____ E-mail address: _____

Payment: _____ Check payable to **Love Language LLC** _____ Money order

MAIL TO: Love Language™ LCC, 2111 E. Santa Fe, #268, Olathe, KS 66062

Canadian Orders: Add $5.00 per item for shipping/handling.
International Orders: Add $10.00 per item for shipping/handling.
Prices, shipping and handling charges subject to change without notice.

Love Language™ products are also available for credit card purchase at

www.babysingandsign.com

BABY SING & SIGN™ Music CD

1. **Clap Your Hands** (Ruth Crawford Seeger)
   Included with permission by the Seeger Family (BMI)

2. **This Is the Mommy** (Anne Meeker Miller)

3. **Mommy Go 'Round the Sun** (Based on Edith Fowke's "Sally Go 'Round the Sun')
   Included with permission by the Writers' Union of Canada

4. **Doggie, Doggie** (Anne Meeker Miller)

5. **Roll the Ball** (Traditional)
   Included with permission by GIA Publications

6. **The Walking Song** (Traditional/lyrics by Anne Meeker Miller)

7. **Where's Baby?** (Anne Meeker Miller)

8. **Miss Mary Jane** (Traditional)
   Included with permission by Harvard University Press

9. **The Little Cats Go Creeping** (Traditional)
   Included with permission by GIA Publications

10. **Bunny Boogie** (Anne Meeker Miller)

11. **Charlie Over the Water** (Traditional)

12. **My World** (Anne Meeker Miller)

13. **Skye Boat Song** (Traditional)

14. **Lady, Lady Lullaby** (Traditional)
    Included with permission by GIA Publications

Produced by Anne Meeker Miller and Kelly Werts
Engineer: Kelly Werts/Werts Music
Mastered by Chris Crabtree
Vocals: Anne Meeker Miller
Guitar: Kelly Werts
Bass: James Albright
Rhythm: Paul Van Sickle
Violin: Kelly and Molly Werts
Other instrumentals: Kelly Werts
Special Vocals: Lana Herman, Hayley and Megan Martin, Darren Meyers, Dan, Greg, Kevin
   and Andy Miller, Marcheta Pearson, Cora Powers, Rick Fisher and Pam Williamson

Special thanks to Kelly Werts for his exceptional musicianship, technical direction and
moral support throughout the recording process.